Manifesto
Addressed to the President of the United States from the Youth of America

Edited by Alan Rinzler

MANIFESTO
ADDRESSED TO THE
PRESIDENT OF THE UNITED STATES
FROM THE YOUTH OF AMERICA

The Macmillan Company
Collier-Macmillan Ltd., London

The Macmillan Company
866 Third Avenue, New York, N.Y. 10022
Collier-Macmillan Canada Ltd., Toronto, Ontario

Library of Congress Catalog Card Number: 71-123885

First Printing

PRINTED IN THE UNITED STATES OF AMERICA

Contents

Editor's Introduction

I was born in 1938. People my age (and older) grew up during a time when things appeared to be a lot simpler. Our parents had just endured a great economic depression which created profound anxiety about such fundamentals as food and shelter and what these meant in terms of self-worth, manhood, freedom. Then we lived together through a horrendous World War which seemed to threaten civilization and all humanistic evolution to date, in fact a holy war for survival. From our earliest experience, therefore, we assumed that money was essential for personal and public self-love and stability; and that violence was the necessary arm of goodness versus the forces of evil. Or any other Opposition.

Many of our parents, in addition, were still struggling up from the lower, often immigrant classes, into the safety of the American Dream. We had to do better, of course, but the route was clear. Certainly there were many obstacles to overcome, but options were defined, choices limited. There was no question about the necessity of money and violence: materialism and aggressive-competitive achievement. Life was conceived as a struggle, the daily means of which, however unsatisfying, justified An End. Individual and collective fulfillment was elusive and very far in the future. In the meantime, specific traditional roles were the only valid structures and would someday, somehow, become the instruments of both personal completion and collective reform. And these roles were quite clear. We knew perfectly well what it was to be a child, a student, a young man or woman, a wife or

husband. We were also happy to accept existing societal institutions—familial, spiritual, educational, political, economic—as given forms within which we
could define ourselves, our work and whatever change
or reform we would eventually determine expedient for
all of us within that framework.

For me at least, this meant being a good student,
attempting leadership within preexistent social, artistic
and political school groups, going to "the best" college,
getting married, raising a family and "making a living"
within a hallowed and highly traditional communications industry which in turn is part of an overall politi-
cal-corporate-cultural Establishment. Nor would there
have been any question about going into the Army had
not early fatherhood fortunately provided exemption.
Whatever vague malaise or discontent my generation
experienced during its adolescence in the fifties was
expressed unilaterally through tangential life-styles or
personal, usually self-destructive acts of violence or,
most important, by first contact with another funkier
real America—Black America—through the beginnings
of a spiritual, cultural and ultimately political revolution known as rock and roll.

Fine. That's my trip, as it is now said, and I'm en-
joying it very much. Because it's been so easy, really,
moving along a step at a time, playing certain roles,
fulfilling certain expectations, achieving definite goals.
Because the kind of limited and basically self-denying
satisfaction provided within these traditional premises
is quite tangible. And because being born since 1938,
say in 1948 or 1958, has been in so many ways far
more difficult. Which is what this so-called *Manifesto
Addressed to the President of the United States from
the Youth of America* is all about.

Things, as the great African writer Chinua Achebe
writes, have fallen apart. The assumptions inherited

from that great depression and holy war have been tested these twenty-five years and proven wanting. Those institutions which were alleged to perform certain necessary functions have proven failures. The academy, the corporation, the government have not—from purely pragmatic evidence—been able to fulfill our personal or collective needs. In fact, it now appears, to our dismay and alarm, that these structures may by their inherent nature be diametrically opposed to precisely that commonweal they were meant to promulgate and insure.

Moreover, as these institutions have lost their validity, individual roles have concurrently become far less easy to define. Both the passage of time and the tremendous acceleration of informative communication all over this global village have revealed much new truth about how the society of nation-states propagates the interests of its rulers through violence, oppression and the suspension of those ethical values it purports to further for its own people; how corporate, academic and cultural institutions condition their citizenry to contribute to these goals; and what this implies for all of us as individuals responsible first of all to our own self-definition (vis-à-vis self-love, morality, self-purification, holiness) and also to all other life on this planet.

As a result, growing up today can no longer be the traditional act of honoring one's ancestors and carrying things on as they are. Being young no longer can mean choosing from a limited deck of ready-made options or roles, but rather something far more strenuous, more demanding and—from my vantage point at least—more frightening. More frightening because all previous bets are off. We can no longer affirm any handed-down roles or values; we can no longer trust the validity or ulterior motives of our sacred academic, spiritual institutions; we can no longer believe that corporate capitalism in America is really for the benefit of all; we can no longer assume that our government really represents or acts in behalf of our personal or collective well-being. All of which puts a tremendous new burden on each individual, particularly those young people who have not yet nor are likely to ever accept any of those bogus conventions their elders proselytize out of habit, cowardice or ignorance of true self-interest.

What this means is simply freedom and responsibility. Freedom to find one's true self, to break through any superimposed parental or societal conditioning and discover our real identity. And responsibility once this precious individualism is revealed—with all its indigenous needs and values—to act.

Who are we and what will we do? These are questions each of us must answer for ourselves. But at least one thing this Manifesto reveals is that if life itself on this planet is to survive, we can no longer avoid asking these questions, nor can we assume that any of them have been or will be answered for us. Once we come as close as possible to knowing the who of us and the how, we must then move in our way—each of us in our different way—toward the fulfillment of this true self and whatever it can subsequently contribute toward the best interests of all life.

This book represents one manifestation of new freedom and responsibility. It has been compiled on the occasion of the 1970–71 White House Conference on Children and Youth by asking young people from all over the country to express themselves, their immediate local condition and their sense of present and future responsibility for whatever Establishment with or by which they feel most involved, hopeful, oppressed.

The result is far from a complete portrait. But it is a collection of twenty-nine honest young voices from a broad spectrum of opinion, background and location.

For this we are grateful to: Dennis Hale, who put us in touch with many contributors from the so-called left; to William F. Buckley, Jr., Arnold Steinberg and David Frank, who helped us locate the young conservatives and libertarians; to Vine Deloria, Jr., and Stan Steiner, who recommended the Indian contributors herewith; to Elizabeth Sutherland Martinez for her Chicano friends and neighbors; and to Gwen L. Kimbrough, who helped us find young black voices.

One final observation, writing here as the bombs explode around us this spring of 1970 in the United States of America: Everything—as it is written in the Bible, the Kabbalah, the Bhagavad Gita, the teaching of Lao Tzu, the I Ching and the seminal documents of nearly every spiritual body of thought—is both very complicated and very simple. The complexities of our predicament are rampant in each of the voices that follow. But on one point we concur. And that is the necessity for freedom, self-discovery, self-definition . . . and the necessary responsibility each of us then has for our brothers and sisters and for all life on this planet Earth. For this reason I've concluded our Manifesto with "The Unanimous Declaration of Interdependence" written by the Ecology Action group and others from the San Francisco Bay Area. The ramifications of this document are myriad—forcing us to reconsider nearly every aspect of who we are and how we function individually and as a species—but its gospel is simplicity itself: survival. Not Youth survival, or United States survival, or even Human survival . . . but the naturally evolving survival and harmonious perfection of all Life in the Divine Cosmos.

—Alan Rinzler

Hank Adams

A twenty-seven-year-old Assinoboine–Sioux from Poverty Flats, Fort Peck Reservation, Montana, Hank Adams grew up in Indian communities throughout western Washington State, where he now leads the Survival of American Indians Association in their struggle on the riverbanks and in the courts to protect historic salmon fishing rights once guaranteed by United States treaties. Editor of the newsletter *The Renegade*, he formerly worked as a researcher, writer and lobbyist in Washington, D.C., for the National Congress of American Indians and the National Indian Youth Council, then as director of the Quileute Tribe's poverty program. A leading figure in the Poor People's Campaign in 1968, he made a remarkable showing that year as an inactive Congressional candidate. More recently Mr. Adams has been involved in the formation of a national Indian Cultural Center on Alcatraz Island and is also writing a book to be published by Holt, Rinehart and Winston.

❧❧❧❧❧❧❧❧❧❧❧❧❧❧❧❧❧❧❧❧❧❧❧❧❧❧❧❧❧❧❧❧❧❧❧❧❧❧

The American Indian has not been a beneficiary of this nation's strengths, but rather a continuing victim of its weaknesses—and our own. Dispossessed of a continent and confined to the unnatural existence of the reservations, the Indians' lives, remaining lands and other resources were entrusted unto the care and control of the United States government to be administered in our "own best interests," without Indian interference.

Indians did not become citizens under the Fourteenth Amendment in 1868 because of the sovereign character of our tribes and our owing allegiance to them. The granting of citizenship to all Indians in 1924, however, brought no material change to Indian lives. Subsequent years have brought forth still greater misery, despair and sterile conditioning.

The national mood has periodically been such as to demand a commitment in public policy toward alleviating and dispelling chronic problems that, in the public mind, have been endemic to the Indian personality and ecological condition. The national maturity necessary for devising effective programming and rendering productive assistance, nevertheless, has always been lacking.

Today the Indian people approach the future with the most negative economic, education and employment rates in the nation. As reformist Ralph Nader wrote in 1956 and appropriately repeated in 1969 Congressional testimony, Indians remain "a people without a future."

Indians retaining tribal affiliations—which federal agencies generally count as their self-ascribed service populations—number substantially fewer than 500,000 people. Significantly, Indians have owned and still possess many resources that have not been available to millions of other impoverished people in urban slums, ghettos and rural areas. Among these: the tribes collectively own 2 percent of United States territory, or 55 million acres of land containing valuable mineral, timber, water and fishery resources; they have more than $250 million in the United States Treasury; and they are serviced by a federal Indian program currently budgeted at $525 million annually (this does not include state and private programs).

The resources and services, however, are not distributed uniformly among the native American Indian populations. Poverty is. Present federal programming may offer little more to the Indian future than poverty in perpetuity—and bureaucratic positions for white men. With properties estimated as valuing nearly $10 billion, apart from further improvements and economic exploitation, Indians have been consigned to a role of being wealthy landholders, while remaining functional paupers.

The reasons, oddly, are more obvious than inexpli-cable.

Public policy and federal programming throughout the national history have always manifested ambivalent, contradictory social and political attitudes toward In-dians.

One continuing hope for Indians has been the judi-cial standard arrived at early in the life of the nation by the United States Supreme Court. Justice John Marshall's declaration that Indians occupy a legal dimension as political sovereigns—being, in the first in-stance, independent nationals possessing the rights of nations and original title to the soil—was difficult to reconcile with public attitudes, which ranged from holding that Indians were social inferiors to doubting if they were even possessed of sufficient "human traits" to argue against a policy of outright extermination and disposal.

The objectives common to subsequent national In-dian policy thus became those of reducing or extin-guishing the force of Indians' natural and distinct political rights, and of "elevating" their "social and human character" from that of "Indians."

The features common to the several hundred treaties between the federal government and the tribes were the cession of Indian land title to the United States and the tribes' declaration of dependence upon the United States in exchange for its protection. These documents established the doctrine for the federal gov-ernment to assume complete political control over the lives and properties of Indian tribes and individuals, control to be exercised, in the first instance, by the Congress.

Functional control over Indian lives, however, has been exercised most fully by the Bureau of Indian Affairs, established in 1849 in the Department of Interior after being originally in the War Office. The primary function of the BIA was to undertake the final civilizing measures upon the Indian population through the dispensation of goods and welfare services provided gratuitously by the Congress or under the provisions of the various treaties.

The Indian Bureau's major responsibilities shifted to the management of Indian properties and funds when the Congress decided in the 1880s that tribal lands should be divided up and allotted in trust to individual Indians. It was agreed that breaking up tribal communities to commit all Indians to agrarian life would have an "overwhelming civilizing effect"—caring nothing for the respective tribal experiences and ignoring all the implications of the industrial revolution.

Ensuing exploitation of Indian vulnerability resulted in the loss of two thirds of reserved lands from Indian ownership before Congress decided, in 1934, to take the corrective action necessary. Further land allotments were then prohibited. Consequently, most Indian property owners today are over thirty-five years in age. Since then, 13.5 million acres of land have passed into divided ownership through lines of inheritance—with federal restrictions upon approved use so extreme as to totally remove this acreage from productive utilization and benefit either by the multiple owners, individual interests or tribes.

The lease of Indian lands to non-Indians has been the most common form of BIA property management. In 1967 this was reflected by non-Indians securing only

56.6 percent of the total $105,200,000 gross income drawn from Indians' nonirrigated agricultural–range lands. Non-Indians grossed $52,400,000 in lease of just 2.13 million acres of select Indian agricultural lands out of the total 44.2 million acres in use. Irrigated lands present similarly distressing figures.

Simply stated, Indians are now making their major investments in their least productive lands at a much lower rate of return than that which accrues to non-Indians who lease the Indians' most productive agricultural lands.

The unemployment rate among Indians is reportedly 40 percent; yet 79,000 Indians, or 60 percent of the Indian labor force, are presently unemployed or under-employed, according to confidential figures provided last year to the Bureau of the Budget. The BIA anticipates the reservation labor force will, at a 1 percent rate of annual increase, number 140,000 by 1973—but realistically assumes "no improvement in employment rates" in its program projections for the next five years.

The BIA's Industrial Development Program is cited as its major program for creating reservation employment. The IDP accounted for less than two hundred new jobs annually in its first decade of operation, and its total payrolls amounted to a per capita income increase to reservation Indians of slightly more than $10 —during a period in which national per capita income had increased over $700. In 1966 the BIA declared it had attracted twenty-six new industrial plants to Indian areas to create 1,700 new jobs. In 1968 it was disclosed that these plants had produced only 319 jobs, generating an average annual wage of only $2,912.

Programs in employment assistance, relocation and vocational training are centrally designed to remove more than thirty thousand Indians from the reservations each year; there is no comparable assistance in

training or job development if the same persons desire
to stay on the reservation. Programs that tend to serve
large family units generally provide considerably less
income than the $3,120 average income that institu-
tional vocational trainees were found to be earning
three years after completion of training, according to
a BIA justification for funding requests last year.

The results of BIA job development programs do not
compare favorably with the bureau's own internal
growth. Last year the BIA and the Public Health
Service–Indian Division asked Congress to approve
923 new permanent positions for their combined employee structures; the bureau alone estimated it will
need 6,252 additional employees by 1973—having advanced to 16,177 by mid-1967. PHS–ID entered the
fiscal year of 1968 with 6,694 authorized permanent
positions.

Significantly, in the same period Indian family income, drawn primarily from nonfederal sources, increased 18 percent to $1,600 per year; federal expendi-
tures for Indians increased by 400 percent. If paid directly to 400,000 Indians, current expenditures would
provide more than $6,500 per five-member family unit.

Present programming is actually not keeping pace
with growing problems. The existence and demands of
one program only attest to the failures of others. Under
current dropout rates, 95,000 of the present 162,000
Indian elementary and secondary school students can
be expected not to complete high school. Though only
16,000 out of 57,000 housing units now designated as
substandard are considered renovatable, only a mere
2,400 new housing starts annually are programmed.
Health and disease problems are becoming more visible
in their severity rather than becoming radically improved.

What needs to be done? The present Congress and

Administration are fully committed to errors of the past and are primarily engaged in carrying forward the burdensome foundations for continuing failures. The Indian leadership is so enveloped by fear and insecurity that they protectively embrace and defend these foundations, while damning their manifest errors.

There must be qualitative reform of the federal–Indian relationship now with consequent commitment to effect the dramatic changes such reform requires.

The Bureau of Indian Affairs should be abolished prior to 1976, in order that a third "century of dishonor" may not begin. We may, assume that all its employees are qualified to secure honest jobs in other pursuits.

A new agency, headed by a Cabinet-level director, to sustain the federal–Indian relationship should be established in the Executive offices of the President. This unit should have at least one representative selected by each tribal unit in the nation, including an ordinate number of Aleuts and Eskimos, and a professional staff not exceeding the number of native American staff (apart from clerical support). Its principal functions would be to provide and administer community development grants to the local-tribal governments and to contract with various Indian communities and urban organizations for the conduct of essential services programs. It could redirect funds to priority needs and programs of local communities through absorbing the present funding levels while effecting elimination of the related programs. The full dimensions of its role would be established by collective Indian determination.

Revision of the trust relationship is required to eliminate restrictive aspects while continuing its beneficial elements. Congress should enact legislation to continue tax exemptions for Indian properties and income de-

rived directly therefrom until the year 2000, and prohibiting alienation of any and all properties from
Indian ownership for the same period of time. With
these provisions in force, the status of trust and its
management responsibilities could be dispensed with.

Trust funds now held in the United States Treasury
could conceivably be consolidated under some form of
corporate trust to provide a continuous investment and
limited-development fund for enabling collective utilization and circulation of Indian monetary resources.
Such a nationally consolidated fund could enable their
conversion for collateral use or working capital under
reasonable interest and return rates, as opposed to their
present nonuse.

Essentially, this nation must now affirm its good
faith with the Indian people and its own spirit of government by respecting and providing legal support to
the tribal communities in their distinct political and
cultural dimensions. In a sense, we need a chance to
unify the institutions that govern our lives through a
system of good local government drawn in the context
of our tribal-reservation existence—and granted positive standing within the systems of both federal and
state governments.

Given command of our own resources and afforded
appropriate assistance, we will have the means and
mechanics to bring economic solutions to our economic
problems. We can develop processes of education—
drawing upon the strengths of cultural diversity and
free from the design of cultural devastation—that will
allow us to remain at home in our communities while
providing us with the academic advancement and social
mobility necessary to take up residence within any element of American life. We could bring security to our
families through adequate employment and income for

heads of families, enabling them to meet the personal needs and social concerns of all family members.

The real question is whether this post-Columbian nation can summon the integrity and courage to abort the maladapted mission of the Bureau of Indian Affairs and abolish it. If not, there is small chance of advancing solutions to problems in any major sphere of concern. If not, this post-Apollo nation will have lost the benefit of its most creative human experiences and will continue to give but misguided direction to the destiny of its pre-Columbian people.

Nita Jo Gonzales Aleman

A recently married twenty-year-old high school graduate, Mrs. Aleman was "exposed quite early to the fact
that our country is not the land of gold and equality I
was taught in school. I am now traveling through the
migrant stream which has shown me all the facets of
discrimination and the problems my *raza* must suffer.
I will continue writing and working toward the rebuilding of my people and our *Aztlan*. . . ."

✦✦

Signs proclaiming BLACK POWER, CHICANO POWER,
POWER TO THE PEOPLE, NATIONALISM, REVOLUTION and
INSURRECTION are samples of what has erupted from
coast to coast and sea to sea as the world's youth declares itself human. And through the curtain of discontent that surrounds our country's schools, campuses
and slum areas, a face emerges. The face of a too-long-
silent race; a face whose brown windows quietly reveal
a heritage three hundred years old; a face whose hum-
ble expression vividly confesses twenty thousand years
of existence; a brown face that lays claim to the fact
that we are a *mestizo* race. Indian mother and Spanish
father brought forth a breed of *mestizos* known to the
mentality of this society as a hyphenated citizen; the
label reads MEXICAN–AMERICAN. We, the new breed
of *mestizos*, would be the "niggers" in a land that we
nursed and coddled, watching, protecting, even at the
cost of the blood of our wives, husbands, sons and
daughters, with the hope and justification that our
grandchildren would benefit from the fruit our lives
and labor would reap from *mi tierra* (my land).

Then the white sea of maggots came and tore the yet

unweaned child from my *raza's* (race) bosom, and on its valleys, mountains and plains flew a foreign body, a body of red, white and blue. But that has passed, and progress has lengthened the life span and enabled the busy housewife to give more time to her church activities. Now man, a white man, has claimed the moon god for the good old U.S.A. Yet in the fields, the mines and the factories children of Zapata, Villa, Quetemoc and Che crave a glass of milk or a piece of bread. And in the hearts and souls of the second, third and fourth generation Chicano a continual anger seethes, a growth of bitterness and sometimes hate for the government and the people who shove us under the mat only to call us out to sell Fritos or to die to save a *gringo* major in a war where promises and treaties are silenced by machine gun fire, the smell of death and cries of anguish.

As the earth continues its revolution around the sun, science prepares for man's first step on Mars, local police brush up on their riot procedures and Chicanos throughout the Southwest venture into a new era of movement. As my *raza* glances back over the scenes at the close of Act I, we recall the march of three thousand migrant workers from Delano to Sacramento, California—a march that emphasized the rights denied to the migrant worker. Demands were made—demands for better housing, better wages and the freedom to be a Chicano, a man.

Fifteen thousand Chicanos march together at a Los Angeles Blow Out. Fifteen thousand walk out to dramatize that we are no longer second-class citizens who own nothing but a name, a language, a heritage—our keys to the doors of economy, education, individualism and equality.

Thirty are arrested in Del Rio, Texas, for exercising their right to the freedom of speech, a right that we are asked to respect, a right that the present-day law enforcers do not uphold. And so one week later two thousand Chicanos respond to the Establishment's blunder by demonstrating that our *raza* has had enough, and cries of *"Ya basta"* ("We've had enough") still linger in the atmosphere.

A walkout of West High School students in Denver followed by a confrontation with the police set the stage, and four days and four nignts ·belong to the Chicano community. During that short period of time, a Chicano *barrio* dared to lift its head face-to-face with its oppressor.

The last of March, 1969, and the beginning of April were witnesses to the harmony of the voices and *gritos* (yells) which at one time or another proclaimed to the city fathers "Chicano Power." They were heard together with chants of *"Unidos venceremos"* ("United we shall overcome"), letting the sound of their proclamation ring across the Southwest. From the *barrio*, the school and the campus, eighteen hundred representatives from all Chicano youth organizations heard the call for unity and eighteen hundred came when the Crusade for Justice sponsored the first Chicano Youth Liberation Conference. After four days of constant discussion, deliberation, songs, dances and *actos,* eighteen hundred joined forces and announced to the oppressors of our people that *Aztlan* (the name given to the land north of Mexico by the Aztecs) would live again in *"El Plan Espiritu de Aztlan."* ("The Spiritual Plan of Aztlan").

Mi Raza declares to you, "Columbia," our preamble of independence.

EL PLAN ESPIRITU DE AZTLAN

In the Spirit of a new People that is conscious not only of its proud historical heritage, but also of the

Brutal "Gringo" invasion of our territory, we, the Chicano inhabitants and civilizers of the Northern land of their birth and concentrating the determination of our people of the sun, Declare that the call of our blood is our Power, our responsibility, and our inevitable destiny.

We are Free and Sovereign to determine those tasks which are justly called for by our house, our land, the sweat of our brows, and by our hearts. Aztlan belongs to those that plant the seeds, water the fields and gather the crops, and not the foreign Europeans. We do not recognize capricious frontiers on the Bronze Continent.

Brotherhood unites us, and love for our brothers makes us a people whose time has come and who struggles against the Foreigner "gavacho" who exploits our riches and destroys our culture. With our heart in our hands and our hands in the soil, we Declare the Independence of our Mestizo Nation, We are a union of Free Pueblos. We are Aztlan.

Por la Raza Todo

Fuera de la Raza Nada

The above declaration is supplemented by a step-by-step plan to restore my people's dignity and the individualism our ancestors once relished. The first step of *El Plan* is nationalism. Our *jefitos* and *jefitas* (parents) held onto the old way, saving our *raza's* traditions and values of life from total destruction by the technical, competitive society now in existence. But no longer are the youth of *la raza* going to humbly accept the indignities and psychological destruction of our people.

Elementary school children, as well as students in secondary schools and colleges, are now demanding that the history and heritage of our people be taught in their schools. We are demanding that the Treaty of Guadalupe be upheld and bilingual education be put into effect, not just on a college or high school level, but from the very start of formal education.

We no longer wish to feel that we can't speak our mother tongue in school for fear of expulsion and that we are inferior because the *teacher* is "culturally deprived" and is unable to pronounce our names correctly. Chicanos everywhere are now beginning to stir as our self-identity is being restored.

Food co-ops, cultural centers and our own newspapers are the tools young Chicanos are using to bring about a change in their lives across the Southwest. Through these devices the Chicano organizations of *Aztlan* hope to become economically independent of this society. We hope to build an economy of our own that will bring life back into our economically drained communities. We toil for a future where our families, who move with the crops for survival, will find the means necessary to sustain life on land of their own; a future in which *la raza* will not be forced from the frying pan into the fire, moving out of the migrant stream into a rat-infested *barrio*.

When our people make the move to the city, we do not have the technical skill to make a living for our families. We are, therefore, forced into a position where we must receive assistance from the city welfare office. But though our people must receive welfare payments or some form of governmental assistance to survive, we will not be treated as though we are animals. We insist that such assistance is a "right" and not a "privilege."

Too often the city fathers decide that our children will be bused to other schools in the hope that they will assimilate into this "good society." But it is definitely assured that these "underprivileged" children will be unable to keep up with children who have had the advantage of rat-free homes, modern schools, highly up-to-date books and qualified teachers. We demand that our schools be rehabilitated; that the money now spent for busing be used for refurnishing *barrio* schools, hiring Chicano teachers and supplying our school libraries with books relating to *la raza*.

September 16, Mexican Independence Day, was celebrated this year in Denver by a crowd of more than eight thousand, and more than four thousand Chicanos walked out of their schools to bring to the attention of our oppressors that as long as this country and this government refuse to let us breathe, we will take it upon ourselves to struggle to the surface of this "melting pot."

In this manner we are beginning to find our own solutions to the problems that confront and have surrounded us for generations. We submit that our answer to the racism of this society is nationalism. A nationalism that is not of necessity exclusive, but that does let us set our own definitions and our own priorities. A nationalism that strives to be self-sufficient without being imperialistic or exploitative. A nationalism that is named *Aztlan*.

Jim Broadus

Twenty-three-year-old Jim Broadus graduated from
Oberlin College where he was associate editor of *The
Activist* and president of the Young Democrats. Born
in Mobile, Alabama, and now living in Lexington, Kentucky, he grew up waving the rebel flag at beach parties,
then participated in the campaigns of Carl Stokes,
Robert Kennedy and Eugene McCarthy. After working
on pipeline construction, as a playground director, a
Neighborhood Youth Corps counselor and an organizer
for Church Community Service in Lexington ("organizing whites against racism and political impotency"), he
currently reports having a hard time getting back into
"what now seems like a kind of contrived mediocrity
in pluralist politics."

Lexington, Kentucky, in the summer: I am on the
back of a pickup truck with fellow pipeline laborers.
A conversation is started concerning the latest-model
cars. The talk is naturally extended to wealth and status
in general and how one attains them. Eventually "Cowboy," a sixty-year-old man who has been working on
pipelines for the past forty years (and is now earning
the same $1.90 an hour as the rest of us), makes a
comment. It is accepted as a consensus by the men in
the truck: "An *honest* man just can't get ahead."

Oberlin College, Ohio, in the fall: Three hundred
student demonstrators trap a Navy recruiter in his car
for four hours. They are dispersed with tear gas after
high-pressure fire hoses have failed.

Lexington, Kentucky, in the summer: Blacks in this
paradigm of the Old South stage small riots and form
politically significant organizations. Local police re-

spond by ordering a massive supply of riot-control equipment and by doubling patrols in black communities, while crime rates in the rest of the city soar.

Lexington, Kentucky, in the summer: I march with 150 University of Kentucky students to City Hall. We are protesting repressive police tactics and are joined by a hundred townspeople. This is the first time in the university's history that its students have displayed an active concern for the affairs of the surrounding community.

Fort Knox, Kentucky in the winter: A friend of mine is harassed by his officers for distributing an antiwar GI newspaper. The paper is widely accepted by the enlisted men. In the spring, a Lexington soldier will be removed from his job as sentry at the Tomb of the Unknown Soldier and ordered *back* to Vietnam for making an antiwar comment.

Oberlin, Ohio, in the spring: Six thousand caps of mescaline are consumed in two weeks at this college of 2,500 students.

Charleston, West Virginia, in the spring: Thousands of West Virginia miners march on their capital to demand legislative protection against "black lung" disease. The march is against the wishes of their now unrepresentative union. One miner says, "If the goddamn union don't protect us, we'll protect ourselves."

Oberlin, Ohio, in the spring: Listening to WCJW, Cleveland's country-music station, I hear in song of "that crazy war in Vietnam." I notice that my hip friends are beginning to listen to and appreciate country music. Likewise, popular performers are beginning to move into the country idiom. A class-cultural gap is being bridged. From the jukebox in the college snackbar I hear that "You gotta tear it down to build it up."

Each of these little stories represents a personal experience with the widespread discontent now generally recognized in our society. Several different trends in this discontent are definable: hippy/drugs; blacks; student activists; angry labor. While these trends often appear to be divergent at present, they all evidence disgust with current societal conditions. Loosely grouped together, they can be discussed as a single counterclass; and, if chance or design coalesces them, they could become a powerful revolutionary force. The mounting evidence of resistance in the armed services, independence in labor movements and militancy in traditionally intimidated welfare recipients (not to mention rumblings of organization among lower-middle-class taxpayers) suggests that this nascent force is approaching adolescence, with all of adolescence's spontaneous outbursts and internal struggle. Adolescence, as we all know, is soon followed by maturity.

Alfred Marshall wrote that "the two great forming agencies of the world's history have been the religious and the economic. Here and there the ardor of the military or the artistic spirit has been for a while predominant: but religious and economic influences have nowhere been displaced from the front rank even for a time; and they have nearly always been more important than all the others put together."

The most active counterclass components in recent years have been moved by the religious strain: protests against the immorality of our war on Vietnam, against the injustice of our economic institutions, against the structural restrictions on personal liberty and against the general dehumanization of our technological society. This neoreligious trend has also gained currency in the tension-related response toward mysticism, sense experience, witchcraft and psychedelia. The counterclass will not gain effective maturity until economic and religious-like motives operate in concert. In fact, these two forces are beginning to combine in a concern with income distribution and poverty.

At the same time, American policy makers may be caught in a dilemma. On the one hand, the public is demonstrating that it will no longer support seemingly interminable, expensive and morally suspect counter-insurgency wars such as the one in Vietnam. On the other hand, America's prosperity is based largely on the fact that 6 percent of the world's population consumes 70 percent of the world's resources. Third World insurgency movements are ultimately a response to this fact, and if forecasts of population demands on world food supplies are valid, these movements will intensify.

The success of Third World insurgency movements could require radical alterations in present American domestic institutions. As John Wilkinson has pointed out, "[our] neo-colonialism (which instead of occupying troops, relies on drawing governments, often military dictatorships, into the American economic network) is probably very fragile. A large-scale insurrection in Latin America could result in revolutionary changes in the U.S." However, United States action to circumvent world insurgency would probably require historically unprecedented domestic repression. In practice, policy makers have generally approached this dilemma by hedging with "limited" holding tactics on each front.

We remember the old "war on poverty" as such a hedge, and more recently some form of "black capitalism" has been pushed as the biggest source of miracles since black magic. Yet in trying to soften their burden at home by appearing to "eliminate" poverty, policy makers are trapped in archaic notions of just what poverty means.

They insist on considering poverty as a problem associated with an undesirable "residual" in our generally "affluent" society. They seem to overlook the fact that in this "overwhelmingly middle-class" country only 25 percent of the population receives an annual income of over $10,000. A rich twentieth of the population receives 15 percent of all the income (and owns over half of all the wealth). For professionals, associating with other professionals, it is easy to forget that only 9 percent of our families make over $15,000 per year. The richest fifth of the population benefits from 41 percent of the country's income, while the poorest fifth receives only 5 percent.

While persons living in officially defined "poverty" may represent a "residual," those living in economic deprivation relative to available resources certainly do not. Half of this nation's population receives barely 20 percent of the income.

The point I am trying to make is that if we are to have any economic justice in our complicated society (and perhaps if we are to have even a bearable stability), policy makers must broaden their conceptions of poverty and economic sufficiency. While "residual" poverty is a moral irritation for "middle-class" policy makers and most student radicals, and a painful problem for the very poor, relative deprivation—inequality —cuts sharply, as we have seen, across the bulk of our populace. Middle-income people (not to be confused with the more affluent "middle class"), struggling to attain the comforts of a middle class in which they mistakenly claim membership, are increasingly more resentful of seeing chunks of their hard-earned incomes diverted to "rehabilitating" the residual poor.

But poverty is not a problem associated with one residual group. Rather it is a problem in the whole economic structure of our society. Residual poverty is only the harshest and most intolerable manifestation of economic inequality. If poverty is to be attacked, then the whole problem must be considered, rather than just its most extreme symptom. Doing this, if it is ever done (which is doubtful), will require policy makers to change their notions of poverty.

Different views of poverty call for often conflicting policy tactics. As sociologist Martin Rein writes, "The different definitions of poverty imply different means to overcome it. What appears to be a concern with 'poverty' is actually a tissue of sometime competing agenda. The term 'poverty' cloaks the competing objectives."

Attacking institutionalized economic inequality would relieve policy makers of the burden of defining the always troublesome and arbitrary "poverty line," for residual poverty—below the present poverty line—would be taken care of in the broader solution of equalization. But it would deprive them of using the phrase as a cloak for the elevation of their own goals in the competing agenda. For policy makers are members of the affluent $10,000-a-year and above middle class with perceptions usually acquired in their particular milieu.

The resulting class restriction has imposed damaging limits on current policy proposals for eliminating "poverty." As economist Harry G. Johnson has written:

> . . . programs for attacking poverty are conceived in middle-class terms and to a significant degree are self-frustrating through concern for the preservation of middle-class values. . . . contemporary thinking about poverty is dominated by the notion of elevating the poor into the middle class . . . and is both seriously handicapped and forced into deviousness by the requirement that this elevation be accomplished in ways consistent with middle-class morality.

This insistence on middle-class morality has been translated into poverty policy by an almost incomprehensible array of restrictions, requirements, eligibility criteria, transfers in kind and social rehabilitation. Such programs are directed at the goals of social control—genteel "law and order" preserving middle-class values and dominance. They are based functionally on the notion of poverty as social pathology, that is, that the poor are a subclass that has been "improperly socialized." Consequently, policies aimed at this poverty are directed at the pathology and must be consistent with social control.

Such policy is formally justified by the contention that deviance from middle-class public norms is the primary problem associated with poverty. More informally, they are defended by a notion held in our Western culture that comes from Aristotle, Augustine, Aquinas and the antiabolitionists, namely, that some men are inferior and should therefore, by natural right, be ruled. Since the affluent middle class (25 percent of our population) owns the economic and political machinery of control, they reason that it must be the rest who are inferior and who ought to be ruled. If a man expects to be "elevated" from poverty, it seems, he must also expect to adopt a middle-class attitudinal and behavorial pattern.

One currently popular approach for reducing this prerequisite for economic welfare is a program of direct income transfers, such as a negative income tax or a guaranteed minimum income. If such programs are instituted, however, it is a good bet that they will be "forced into deviousness" in the interest of continued or extended social control.

The welfare program pushed by President Nixon is of this mold, but it guarantees far too little—just about half the income officially defined as the poverty level—and its work incentives are still directed toward control. A good minimum income program could offer the important advantage of equalizing distribution of the national income, but Nixon's has such a meager cutoff line that it should have little redistributive effect. Nor is there any indication that the program will be financed by a redistributive tax scheme—in other words, the middle-income group will not escape the squeeze.

Nixon's plan might prove useful, however, in breaking the ice for a more meaningful minimum-income program. It could redirect attitudes and open minds to more extensive redistribution that would directly benefit the tax-burdened population massed around the national median income. But this has yet to be seen, and policy is still being directed at the most visible symptom, with the problem of economic inequality remaining untouched. With a more encompassing and just notion of poverty, policy makers could inject a new sense of security and fairness into our economy. This would call for a strategy of active redistribution of the national wealth and income.

Some useful policy tactics would be a redistributive income maintenance program (perhaps with a corresponding income ceiling), decreased tax leniency for corporations and foundations, greatly increased inheritance taxes, a broadened concept of the public good with more governmental investment in projects designed to promote it. The possibility that these tactics, by taking from the rich middle class and giving to the poor majority, might injure investment and growth (and consequently the standard of living) is a real one. But policy makers need not use this possibility as a reason for disregarding the equalization strategy; rather they should more carefully study ways of avoiding the risks.

For policy makers the dilemma posed by external and internal pressures remains. If any semblance of democracy is to be achieved in our society, massive repression must be rejected. The hedges are not working. A strategy of equalization through redistribution of wealth and income could be the solution. But surely all this is mental masturbation, for what I am ultimately suggesting is that the powerful middle class give away some of its power, and this is almost a contradiction in terms. History tells us that power is not given away—it must be taken. So the struggle for economic justice must, and will, no doubt, continue.

Jameson G. Campaigne, Jr.

One of the founders of the 50,000-member Young Americans for Freedom, J. G. Campaigne, Jr., is twenty-nine years old and co-owner/editor of an Indiana–Illinois newspaper publishing and printing chain. A 1962 graduate from Williams College, he precipitated a campus uproar by claiming that his fellow students were victims of a de facto brainwashing due to the lack of any conservative faculty members. Now a full-time conservative activist, he is also active in a Chicago black capitalism training program and has helped to found a preschool reading school for black children in that city's west side ghetto. He expects to "see his ideas become institutionalized in the next decade, then switch sides and begin to work for reforming that future conservative establishment."

What is the spectre haunting the young of the Western societies of Europe and North America and those Westernized cultural entities within the Soviet bloc and in the Third World? It is the awareness that life at the philosophical, social and political levels has very little real meaning.

On the *philosophical* level, more than a century of popular man-centered ideologies like positivism, Hegelianism, existentialism and psychoanalytic speculation has seen each reach a dead end. Their novelty and creativity have worn out. Against the tests of experience and analysis, each of these ideological systems possesses the same Achilles' heel. They ignore some element of reality that can disprove the system. Especially ignored are metaphysical questions, even though of recognized validity by, for example, Comte and Marx, because they would render the ideological system impossible.

On the *social* and *political* levels, democratic socialism in the Western societies and undemocratic socialism in the Soviet bloc have ushered in a "tide of bureaucratization. Government jobs offer no opportunity for personal talents and gifts. Regimentation spells the doom of initiative. The young man has no illusions about the future. He will get a job with one of the innumerable bureaus. He will be a cog in a huge machine, the working of which is more or less mechanical. The routine of a bureaucratic technique will cripple his mind and tie his hands. He will enjoy security. But this security will be of the kind that the convict enjoys within prison walls. He will never be free to make decisions and to shape his own fate. He will forever be a man taken care of by other people. He will never be a real man relying on his own strength. He shudders at the sight of the huge office buildings in which he will bury himself." [1] Bureaucracy, the ugly and soulless handmaiden of liberal-collectivist-socialist ideologies so compelling in theory, is the *reality* of those ideologies. The similarity between the rhetoric of von Mises, written in 1944 about the socialist societies before World War II, and contemporary student rhetoric on *both* the right and left, is striking. It indicates the real awareness the young have, and will always have, of the instinctive human desire for individual freedom. That this instinct can be conditioned out of a man by the time he is middle-aged or elderly (perhaps having opted for mere security) is no guarantee that each new generation will not opt for it.

What young people face today, and what constitutes

[1] Ludwig von Mises, *Bureaucracy* (New Haven, Yale University Press, 1944).

a genuine cultural crisis in Westernized societies,[2] is the sure knowledge, based on experience and common sense, that soft and hard socialist-salvationist ideologies, which promise so much for all men, don't touch base with reality. They have little meaning for the young of this age. In practice, also, these ideologies collapse utterly. We see the evidence of this in the wreckage of the Labour government in England, of Marxism-Leninism in the Soviet bloc and of the institutions of the New Deal–Great Society in the United States. In each case, economic and environmental conditions have worsened, in an absolute sense, in direct proportion to the purity and intensity of the socialist remedy applied. Control over production of goods in the Soviet Union has meant inordinately high prices and short supplies of desired goods. In Britain a government egg-marketing board designed to improve the quality and lower the cost of this staple has done the opposite. In America a farm program designed to protect prices and aid the small farmer has made food inordinately expensive for the poor, while virtually wiping out the small farmer. Countless examples are available. All prove that, when institutionalized, socialist ideologies tend to work against the very goals they profess to seek.

Faced with a world run by ideologies that fail as philosophy or ersatz religion, faced with the failure of these ideologies to deliver the goods in the social and political context, young people sensitive to the resulting crisis of unbelief in the old order have turned in two directions.

The New Left is part and parcel of the utopian, gnostic ideology—in upbringing, classroom indoctrination and subsequent intellectuality and activism. They

[2] I omit the civilized Asian nations like Japan and China only for simplicity's sake; they are experiencing the same crisis in the different contexts of their respective cultures.

lash out blindly at the system that mothered them because it doesn't work as parent, professor and preacher said it would. Yet they hew in most respects to the program of their intellectual patrimony—the sixty-year intellectual-political movement of the Intercollegiate Society of Socialists and the League for Industrial Democracy, and its subsequent offspring, the ADA, CORE, the NAACP and power centers in the many labor union and academic-governmental bureaucracies. From the beginning the characteristic feature of the New Left "was that it had neither new ideas nor plans. They called their action a youth movement precisely because they lacked any program which they could use to give a name to their endeavors. They espoused entirely the program of their parents. They did not oppose the trend toward government omnipotence and bureaucratization. Their revolutionary radicalism was nothing but the impudence of the years between boyhood and manhood. It was the phenomenon of a protracted puberty." [3] Von Mises speaks of German youth prior to World War II living in the same sort of government-corporate-labor union state created by socialists that we see today to a similar degree in Western societies and in the Soviet bloc. Hence, a similar radicalism. In the Germany of that day, the disillusionment and radicalism led to Communist gangs fighting Nazi gangs, and eventually to world war.

In the United States of this day, however, there is a New Right as well as a New Left. And that New Right is committed to scholarship and political activity within traditional bounds. It is committed to those principles of liberty and political truth that animated the conception of this country by its founders, and is conservative of them. It is not conservative of today's status quo.

[3] Von Mises, *loc. cit.*

The New Right has been for the most part outside and in opposition to the ideologies of socialist utopia. It believes that philosophy and theology are means to comprehend all of reality, rather than a blueprint to re-shape it. It opposes the institutionalization of massive bureaucracies whose common function is to make real the blueprint of the ideology—to redistribute wealth and status, control the means of production toward ideological ends and purge the national soul of non-socialist sentiments such as patriotism, religious pre-suppositions, regional characteristics and so on.

At the philosophical level, the right has held to, and *renovated,* the Greek and Christian conceptions of man and nature—in the metaphysical as well as the political sciences. Unlike the adherence to closed systems on the left, the approach of those on the right has been essen-tially Augustinian. It has refused to wrap up all the meaning of human existence within the gates of the City of Man. The realms of truth, beauty and goodness —as in the Greek and Christian break with earlier cos-mological civilizations—remain separate provinces, from which some perspective on human existence can be gained.

The result of this essentially philosophical attitude is a bias against political structures as the be-all and end-all of human endeavor. A desire to maximize lib-erty and personal responsibility in the social and politi-cal realms follows from the right's philosophical under-standing of the nature of man. He is capable of both good *and* evil, of beauty *and* ugliness, of truth *and* willful untruth, of charity *and* selfishness. Man rarely approximates moral perfection. Therefore, rather than have a bureaucratic state composed of flawed men try-ing and failing to remake the nature of other men and society (the Chairman Mao cult), those on the right leave that responsibility to the individual, and to God.

Along with this philosophical understanding has developed a literature in economics and political science that has demonstrated that enterprise economics within a limited government is the most efficient and humane of social paradigms. And at the same time—from Böhm-Bawaerk through von Mises to today's "Chicago School" of economics and "Voegelin-Strauss School" of political science—it has mortally crippled the credibility of socialist economics and political science.

The right sees the intellectual merit of the traditional Western conception of man and the incompleteness and fanaticism of the socialist-utopian ideology. Why then is the world in the sway of the ideologues? The answer to that is rather simple.

To achieve power, the ideology of democratic socialism married organized labor and conceived a welfare constituency. These three vested interests, with other temporary allies like the American South and ethnic groups who have responded to special appeals, have extorted both status(as in the case of the socialist intellectual) and a disproportionately high standard of living (as in the case of union bosses and some rank and file). They benefit from legislation granting them monopoly powers in many labor markets. They extort from the general public, especially the poor and middle-income segments. The welfare constituency finds it possible to remain poor, as the political handmaidens of this trinity of vested interests raise benefits (or at least the promises of benefits). As seen in the writings of Eric Hoffer, the intellectuals have become a virtual ruling class, achieving both psychological and economic satisfaction.

This pattern is virtually identical in all of the Western democracies. In the Soviet bloc, only the names are changed: the bureaucracy, army, members of the Communist Party (less than 10 percent of the population) and a few other special groups like athletes and scientists get the economic privileges and status.

The lust for power by the utopian-socialist-gnostic intellectual creates further problems. Those of the New Right have experienced them in classroom. Here it operates to exclude anticollectivist ideas and professors, creating de facto indoctrination in the schools. The socialism of the New Left radicals is, therefore, no accident. It is virtually the only "truth" available in the academy. Thus, the anarchic life-style of the New Left is the *real* expression of its dissatisfaction with the status quo.

On the world scene, the Communist Party of the Soviet Union—*first an intellectual mass movement,* and second perhaps a Russian national expression—has *armed* the Marxist-Leninist version of utopian gnosticism. It has to date, directly or through proxies, exterminated some eighty million people who didn't bow to it. Doesn't this make the National Socialist version of the same gnostic world view—in fascist Germany and Italy—pale by comparison?

What young people are going to want from their leadership in the years ahead is a way out of the double problem created by the ascendency of the socialist ideology.

They need domestic leadership that will break the hold of the ideology on the academy and intellectual elite. They will have to find ways to break up the unholy trinity of vested interests-plus-bureaucracy on the social and political levels.

On the world scene, the armed socialism of the Soviet Union will first have to be contained at all costs. Eventually it must be met and neutralized through a rigorous policy whose strategy is the eventual liberation of the many different captive peoples within the Soviet sphere. The tactics to realize this goal obviously require realism—a healthy sense of practicality. There will be few quick solutions, few shortcuts. Still, they should be organized under a general strategy that will yield no success to the Marxist-Leninist elite of the Soviet bloc. That elite *feeds* on successes! It still maintains power as a result of not having been countered seriously by the non-Communist world, except in spasms of defense and in a half dozen counterrevolutions in relatively unimportant areas of the Third World.

Soviet leadership would be vulnerable to a Western foreign policy that ridiculed its ideology in theory and practical consequences, that poked at soft spots in the system, such as Soviet literary dissent, the restiveness of Soviet and satellite youths, the persecution of Christians and Jews, the loyalty of the bulk of Russians to Russia and not to Communism, and so on. The aim should be to destroy the credibility and legitimacy of the leadership. This is the opening through which our foreign policy should move—for the sake of our self-defense. The hoped-for result, something not inconceivable, is an eventual coup from below—by nationals probably working in concert with Western powers—that would return Russia to the Russians, the Ukraine to the Ukrainians, and so on. To continue our policy of *polite* coexistence, accompanied by periodic acts of appeasement, is to embolden the Soviet elite and hasten the day when we will come to that last resort to survive as a free people—war.

To anyone not part of the intense academic and political effort of the American right, as well as that of European liberal counterparts, during the past twenty years, the idea that any of the foregoing could come to pass undoubtedly sounds crazy, impossible, unreal. But —apart from many people's lack of real knowledge of what the right stands for—is it "impossible"?

A quick look at history dispels the notion that tomorrow must be like today, as today was like yesterday. The 1932 election is a case in point: FDR was elected after campaigning on an Establishment, "Goldwateresque" platform. Two years later he took the country in the opposite direction—*directly* as a result of the permeation of his Administration by American socialist intellectuals.[4] Until sanctioned by the Democratic Party, the socialists had been vastly unpopular throughout their twenty-odd years of intellectual and political work in the schools and churches. The socialist *coup d'état*, so to speak, came as a result of hard (if imperfect) scholarship, intense proselytizing and savvy political bargaining.

Now institutionalized, the New Deal has lasted more than three decades—the average life span of similar sea-changes in political-intellectual direction in American history. The "revolutions" of Jefferson, Jackson and Lincoln bear this out.

Not at all part of today's semi-socialist establishment, the right is everywhere active: (1) in the academy, with original scholarship and influence on graduate students; (2) in politics, with young conservatives winning a surprising number of elections, both as candidates and as organizers, at all levels of government; and (3) at the intellectual level, in the communications industry among those important "secondhand dealers in ideas" of whom F. A. Hayek wrote in his *The Intellectuals and Socialism.*

It has generally taken a generation for the ideas of seminal thinkers to become institutionalized. And once

[4] The best history of the socialist movement in twentieth-century America, as it influenced politics, is *The Democrat's Dilemma*, by Dr. Philip M. Crane (Chicago, Regnery, 1964). Especially apt is Crane's comparison of the Democrats with the Labour Party in England, both having been redirected by the socialists.

part of the social-intellectual fabric, these ideas last at least a generation. There are no seminal thinkers on the left today, but there are on the right.

If the contest between right and left in America and other countries remains one of ideas, without the intervention of force—for example, by the SDS, labor unions in politics, further leftist suppression of non-left ideas by college faculties—then it is fair to say that the last third of this century will see much of what is advocated in this chapter become fact.

Won't that be exciting?

Terry Catchpole

At twenty-nine, Terry Catchpole has been in and out
of the right for the past eight years, "signing on primarily because I enjoyed attacking the New Frontier
Left Establishment and had a certain fondness for individualism in the face of gargantuan government."
He attended the University of Miami and is now
staff writer for a Washington, D.C., satirical group
and free-lances for *The Village Voice*, the *Washington Sunday Star*, *Rapport*, the *National Review*, *Human Events* and *Good Housekeeping*. He has also acted
professionally and directed plays in the Washington
poverty program.

╬╬╬╬╬╬╬╬╬╬╬╬╬╬╬╬╬╬╬╬╬╬╬╬╬╬╬╬╬╬╬╬╬╬╬╬╬

During one of the many recent debates on government appropriations for arts activities, a Midwestern
Congressman asked his House colleagues if a part of
the federal funds in question was to be spent on the
subsidization of poker players, as that pursuit, to some
minds, constitutes an art form. The gentleman's face-
tiousness notwithstanding, his apparent ridicule characterizes the hang-up government officials, whether
House members or White House residents, have when
it comes to policy toward the arts.

Our inherited Puritan ethic has taught that artistic
pursuits, and their appreciation and/or patronage, are
a luxury, and that any creative activity should be primarily utilitarian. Rural womenfolk make quilts for an
eminently utilitarian purpose: warmth. It is only the
well-off who can afford the luxury of appreciating quilts
for purposes of adornment.

This strain of our ethic is rampant within the official
mentality found operating on all levels of the federal

government. Art for art's sake, its patronage, appreciation and subsidy, is a low-priority item and the purely creative individual is a second-class citizen.

Youth today sees things differently. For them, every man is an artist, every street corner is a gallery. They distrust the Arts Establishment as they do the Military Establishment, and they believe outlets for creativity belong to the people just as do outlets for political expression.

These youths are totally turned off by such creations as "arts councils" and "art centers," as these are the antithesis of their spirited belief that every man should be his own "council" and that wherever he may be at the moment is his "center." The music and fashions of these young people are popular, not because of the Establishment's role in making and promoting them, but because the people themselves originated them and because they are so readily accessible to all who want to experience them.

Clearly then these youths are as opposed as their Congressional countryman from the Midwest to the all-powerful Arts Establishment lobbys, those who suck up most of the federal art funds, and have no desire to see a continued government policy of subsidizing a cultural elite. Undoubtedly the Congressman and the kids would have little agreement on what constitutes good art, but it would appear that there is at least a negative concurrence on the matter of approach.

The key to this approach is diffusion—dispersal, decentralization—of the arts. The principle of decentralization has not won unanimous approval when applied to such things as public education in the city of New York, but this should be no reason for government officials not to apply it in the artistic-creative field. Such a program would be cheap, popular and supremely worthwhile; it would return art to its intended function as an essential facet of life experience, and would also demonstrate the government's concern with quality of life, an urgent cause for a majority of those now under thirty, both radical and nonradical.

It is this cause that has been referred to as the "Second American Revolution," and whether or not the first revolution—toward assuring everyone freedom, equality and a shot at prosperity—can ever be fully achieved, it is far enough along for many youths today to be more personally involved with the implications of this achievement, such as it is, than with the achievement itself. They wonder and worry about the portents of the quantity provided by the first revolution, what it means in terms of moral and spiritual values and what abstract intellectual-culture benefits it currently affords, if any.

If Lincoln Center and the National Arts Council are the end creative-artistic results of the first revolution, then the participants in the second revolution see no recourse but a drastic (nonviolent?) rearrangement of aims and purposes. This they have begun to do. And in rejecting arbitrary authority (which is what any Establishment practices), they have rediscovered the essential role of art: to be as much a part of life and the environment as air, water, money and technology.

They have arrived at this point through diffusion of their own art forms. Rock music, the major example, is not an occasional divertissement for this generation, as a trip to the concert hall or a weekly watching of *The Lawrence Welk Show* is an occasional divertissement for older generations. No, rock is omnipresent. It is in the transistor radios carried everywhere, on the jukebox in every bar, on the tape deck in the car, on the stereo at home, in the air, in their bones.

The same phenomenon is to be found in the other art forms popular with this age group: its theater, poe-

try, painting and literature. These forms are everywhere, every day. The result that is emerging from this
cultural explosion is the most energetically creative generation in our history.

The government should now pick up on this success,
not to please the "youth bloc," if such a bloc indeed
exists, but in the interest of a more sensible, valuable
arts policy and a broader, more appreciative audience.
As it stands now, the government is content to give its
annual appropriation to Establishment-stamped-and-
approved creative outlets, and yet each year the Arts
Establishment, in full public view, ritualistically per-
forms its wrenching, tearful psychodrama of tragedy,
woe and crisis.

A sampling of *New York Times* headlines from early
1969 provides an apt scenario for this annual production:

FORD FUND GLUM ON ARTS OUTLOOK

STEVENS AND HECKSCHER DISCUSS FUND CRISIS IN ARTS

ARTS STILL LOSING GROUND TO RISING TIDE OF COSTS

FIVE MAJOR SYMPHONIES SHARE WOES

KENNEDY ARTS CENTER IN NEED OF 15 MILLION MORE

CITY GETS WARNING ON CULTURE FUND CUT

HECKSCHER WARNS ON ART CUTS FOR INSTITUTIONS

BATES LOWRY CALLS BUSINESS TO RESCUE OF THE ARTS

BUSINESS FAILS ARTS, BARR CHARGES

Curtain? Don't believe it. (Not only do you have a
scenario here, but also a good cross-section of the *dra-
matis personae* and an example of how the *Times* can
serve as a playbill for the psychodrama.)

Sure, everybody who receives federal funds wants
more; some even deserve it. This is no blanket con-
demnation of the individual productions that the Arts
Establishment has mounted, nor is it to say that fu-

ture projects are not worthy of our selective support. However, many of the major problems suffered by the Establishment, and which prompt its annual traumas, are built into its own system and could best be worked out between Establishment members, professional mediators and its "oppressors" (unions, tax agents, real estate people, etc.), not with tax dollars.

The President and Congress, in the meantime, should be more concerned with diffusing art as broadly as possible among their constituents instead of continuing to diffuse their constituents' money among the small, select elite of arts projects and arts administrators who always seem to end up getting it. Or, instead of the scenario outlined in headlines above, visualize the following as taking place sometime next spring:

President Nixon strides from his White House Oval Office to stand before a group of reporters gathered in the Rose Garden, awaiting an announcement. The President speaks:

"I am today asking Congress to join with me in launching a bold and innovative program designed to create widespread renewed interest in the arts among the people of this country. I have sent a request to Congress asking for a supplemental appropriation for the Department of Interior's National Park Service budget in the amount of $500,000. It is understood that this fund is to be divided into five equal portions of $100,000 to be added to the budgets of five of our national parks. This money is then to be used by five artists whom I have asked to go to these parks next summer, where they will exercise their creative powers to enhance the beauty of nature's creation with the magnificence of man's creation.

"Each of these five distinguished men has selected the national park he wishes to work in. Allan Kaprow, one of the pioneers in the 'happening' form of theater, has selected Yellowstone Park; Robert Rauschenberg, one of our leading modern painters, will work in Arcadia National Park in Maine; Alvin Ailey, a foremost developer of modern dance techniques, will go to Yosemite National Park; noted environmental painter and sculptor Edward Kienholz will work in Everglades National Park; and the outstanding theatrical producer and director Joseph Papp has selected Mammoth Cave National Park in Kentucky.

"These creative artists will each have a $100,000 share at his disposal, to be used for materials and salaries for those assistants necessary, not to exceed ten apiece. I want to make it perfectly clear that I will place no restrictions on what they may create and have full confidence that these great artists will remain within the bounds of public tastes and will complement, not detract from, the great beauty of these parks. I am sure that Congress will share with me this confidence.

"The purpose of this program is to bring art and the creative efforts of man back into our natural environment. I have nothing at all against museums, as I am sure you are all well aware, but I also do firmly believe that art belongs out among us. It should be reminding us constantly of who we are as a people and as a nation. Before we were a sophisticated society, we were a rugged nation, and it is my hope today that the efforts of these greatly sophisticated artists, within the context of the rugged terrain they have chosen to be their studio for the summer, will result in a harmonious bond of beauty and majesty. Once this Administration has weighed the results of this initial experimental program and examined our options, then we shall decide where next to carry our program to bring artistic creation back into the daily lives of all Americans. Thank you."

All of which is to say that there is a definite role for the President of the United States to play in the artistic activities of the country beyond presenting Ellington in the East Room and now and then tossing a few monetary crumbs to the Arts Establishment. Before the President assumes the mantle of Patron and Provider, he must first think and act. He must take diffusion of the arts as his guiding principle, then have his arts advisor sit down and think of every conceivable way in which to execute this goal.

For example, every town in the country worthy of its name has a post office. Likewise, every one of these towns has at least one aspiring local artist. Now, is there any logical reason why the wall space of the post office must be reserved only for "Wanted" posters and "No Spitting" signs? Of course not. So, an amendment is attached to the next Post Office Department appropriations bill spelling out how each local postmaster shall name a committee (blue ribbon, naturally) of citizens who shall screen and select local artists for rotating exhibitions in the town's post office. In larger cities, this function could be carried out by already existing arts councils.

And if your neighborhood post office can be magically transformed into a part-time art gallery, so can the steps of the building housing local federal offices (most cities have at least a Selective Service office) become a stage for concerts by local musicians, or a nearby military base can provide bands for downtown noontime and evening performance. Natural parks can provide space for summer theater-under-the-stars, produced by amateur actors in the area. Department of Agriculture extension offices can organize fairs and folk festivals in rural areas. All regional federal officials could be provided with guidelines for encouraging local artistic-creative activities. They could also be advised (so the official will spend little time on them himself), and then be instructed to make federal facilities available for these endeavors whenever feasible.

To organize and oversee the foregoing and other activities, the President should name a Federal Coordinator of Arts Activities to the White House staff. Some recent Presidents have had a Special Assistant for the Arts, largely for show value, and usually the assistant was someone closely wedded to the Arts Establishment. The proposed new position, however, while occupied by someone knowledgeable in the arts, would demand a person not tied to any branch of the Establishment, someone more adept in action and organization than in fund raising and Congressional handholding. The gilded position of Presidentially appointed director of the National Arts Council, meanwhile, would either be abolished or reduced to a largely ceremonial post.

The new aide might begin by coordinating the arts activities of various federal and government-related agencies. Currently, at least a dozen separate agencies have some form of arts program, including the Office of Economic Opportunity, the Office of Education, the Smithsonian Institution, the National Gallery of Art, the Department of the Interior, the National Council (and Foundation) of the Arts and Humanities, the United States Information Agency, the Voice of America, the State Department, the Library of Congress, the Public Broadcasting Corporation and the Department of Health, Education, and Welfare. Presently, it would take a monumental effort by officials in any one of these to know what all the others were doing, or for still other agencies to know what is available for their possible use. A federal coordinator could take care of this, *without* developing his own bureaucracy.

He would also serve as the official to whom the Arts Establishment could turn for advice whenever its annual psychodrama hits a snag and who could lend it a restrained helping hand where necessary. He would be the man to develop such projects as "turning over" five national parks to five artists, and he would be available to propose other programs for the President to undertake, all aimed at encouraging the diffusion of the arts.

The President would be well advised to make a start toward this end right within the government. The "dehumanized" condition of the Washington bureaucracy has been discussed—and rightly condemned—to death, but a person of some authority (whether or not the President himself) might begin to rectify this condition. Providing bureaucrats and file clerks with some diversion other than shoptalk, pigeon feeding and savoring the marvels of a homemade peanut butter sandwich during their lunch period might, just might, make their day—and hopefully their personalities—that much more pleasant and the bureaucracy that much more "humanized." Of course, the first to object to any such irrelevancies in government departments would be the top bureaucrats themselves, but the President must begin to exert his authority over this impervious "fourth branch" of government some day; have him declare: Let there be music . . . and murals on those long, drab corridor walls . . . and plays in the underused auditoriums located in almost every sizable government building in Washington, and—well, you get the picture.

By far the most imaginative and creative action recently taken by the government in an effort to enliven the Washington environment was to allow school kids in the area to decorate the wooden fences surrounding construction sites at Lafayette Park and the JFK Center for the Performing Arts. The resulting montage of youthful paintings was vibrantly beautiful and told you that human beings had been here and left their mark; if you didn't care for one mark, you could move along to the next. Together, the paintings were more valuable to more people than anything that is ever likely to be produced *inside* the JFK Center.

Also, the President could make some use of the prestige of his office to set an example of interest in and encouragement for the arts and artists. Some ideas are:

1. Selecting works of a different living American artist to hang prominently—preferably where tourists could view them—in the White House each month. These one-man showings, which must be representative of the broad spectrum of native schools of paintings, would be well publicized and accompanied by festive openings attended by the President and other dignitaries. The White House is presently a repository of magnificent works by American artists of the past— why not the living too?

2. Viewing new American films in the White House in the company of their director, producer, actors or whoever is available, to be followed by a discussion of the film and the work, problems, ideas, etc., of its creators. Presently the President views, together with his family and friends, any film he wishes to see screened in the White House theater, the fare usually consisting of light entertainments and heavy epics. This is fine; nobody is saying the President should alter his personal tastes. But by viewing all varieties of native films, with quality being the prime criterion, and then talking with their creators, the President would be gaining an understanding of the film industry as well as demonstrating to the country that these creative people, and their creations, are worthy of encouragement and patronage.

3. Attending a few of the poetry readings held regularly in the Library of Congress in Washington. I never recall having read of a President attending a poetry reading *anywhere*, and those at the library are exceptional. Moreover, the President would here be experiencing the artist in the artist's milieu.

4. Arranging White House dinner performances by all types of American artists—the new, young and untried as well as the Established Stars. The early 1969 dinner honoring Duke Ellington, and featuring many older jazz stars, was a smashing success. Why not a dinner for Bob Dylan, featuring folksingers, rock performers and other Dylan contemporaries?

Granted, proposals such as White House dinners and Presidential attendance at arts functions may appear to be getting away from the larger goal of diffusing the arts, but it is equally important for the President to fulfill his role of national leader—as long as he has it anyway—by demonstrating encouragement for all forms of creativity and participating fully in arts events. If the President declares his intention of diffusing the arts, then follows this up with encouragement and participation, and if he is an effective national leader, the arts *will* be diffused and the people *will* be motivated to experience them.

Youth will benefit by having available more opportunities and outlets for creativity and by having a more sensitive audience to perform for. Likewise, concurrent de-emphasis of the Arts Establishment and its prestigious seal of approval should result in a changed public attitude that would be more receptive to innovation and new forms of expression.

In short, what the President needs to do is lead. By setting new priorities, diffusion instead of Establishment-approved development, he will have begun the long process of creating a new audience, the mass of people instead of those able to gain entrée to the culture centers. He will be pointing the national awareness toward a conception of art as part of life, rather than as a luxury set apart from day-to-day existence. When this has been accomplished, the President can turn the Kennedy Center into a low-income housing development.

Wilbur O. Colom

A nineteen-year-old student at Howard University, Wilbur Colom is "a product of Mississippi . . . I've felt the cotton field and the ghetto, the KKK and the drugs all-killing. I've woke up in a rooming house where you walked down stairs flowing the piss. I was with Dr. King in Washington, I was with Stokely Carmichael in Mississippi. I've been in jail twelve times in four different states and been beaten five times. I've been an integrationist, a Muslim, a Black Nationalist and a nothing."

⚜⚜⚜⚜⚜⚜⚜⚜⚜⚜⚜⚜⚜⚜⚜⚜⚜⚜⚜⚜⚜⚜⚜⚜⚜⚜⚜⚜⚜⚜⚜⚜⚜

The United States' major internal problem is black people; more specifically, black youth. We are the catalyst for change in this decadent society. Being the most oppressed segment of this society, it is only right that we should hold this position. We are a doubly marginal group: young and black.

The civil rights movement of the early 1960s had more effect on black youth than on whites. The basic organizing was performed by high school and college students. This demanding work in the South impressed two important points on the minds of these young black workers. First, it was realized that white people controlled the nonviolent movement. The movement was totally based on popular opinion, which was controlled by the news media; hence, the movement became dependent on the media—white people. The most dramatic example of the media's control was in the formation of martyrs for the movement. Whites who were killed in the South became the center of attention, while the large number of blacks who died in the struggle were to a large degree ignored. In addition, whites held absolute control of the purse strings of the movement.

The second lesson of the early civil rights movement was that integration was not actually its correct goal. The organizer began to realize that the problem was one of institutional racism rather than simple individual prejudice.

In all, the early civil rights movements demonstrated that the solution to our problems involved an internal look. We realized that white people in the movement more often confused the issues than helped to clarify them. We also began to understand that eliminating individual prejudice was impossible and in fact not even the fundamental problem that faced blacks in America. Racism has been institutionalized in every function of American life: from federal government to local government; from North to South; from employment to education.

During the Johnson regime, the civil rights movement underwent a trend toward nationalism. President Johnson and other political leaders used a great deal of tokenism, giving a false sense of advancement. The appointment of Thurgood Marshall to the Supreme Court is the most outstanding example of this tactic. However, the appointment of a black person here and a black person there did little to advance the black masses as a whole and nothing to mitigate their frustration. Marshall—like Roy Wilkins and many others —owed his position and power to white people and to white people he was responsible. This tokenism, unfortunately, did aid in dividing the black community on the intentions on the white community. Nevertheless, I truly believe that even the most integration-oriented blacks now realize that America will concede as little as possible.

Since the Nixon regime has captured the White House it appears that tokenism has come to an end. Johnson's tactics of subtle racism are being replaced by Nixon's policy of blatant racism. Nixon's appointments to his Cabinet and his proposals for Chief Justice reflect the clear swing he is making to the right. His actions will probably do more to unite the black community than all the talk about black power these past years.

The Nixon regime has not yet encountered any large-scale rebellion in the Northern black ghettos. Rebellion has shifted from the black ghetto to the college and high school communities. The change is logical. The ghetto rebellions were defeated in battle. Also, many of the youths who initiated and carried on the ghetto rebellions are now of college age. Tokenist colleges and universities have admitted a few of the best "street boys." Once inside, these black students demanded that more of their brothers be admitted; more came and the process continued. Hence, the universities receive the elements for revolt, and black studies became the theme of campus rebellion. But unquestionably, the more astute students realize that this is only a short-term goal in connection with making a black educational system function and promote blackness.

The revolt that originated in the colleges has also moved rapidly to the high schools. The school has become the center of protest, as were the ghetto streets only a short time ago. One reason for this is that most youths are now in school. But more important is the realization by black students that they must create their own education if any progress is to be made toward total freedom.

The military is normally considered the most stable element in a fascist state. But the true test of the depth of our unrest can here be estimated. If a youth today is not in school, he is either unhealthy, in jail, or in the armed forces. But during the last few years the armed services have begun to reflect the frustration of black youth. Confrontations at numerous camps have been reported in the media. Only last year the Marines began allowing black soldiers to wear Afros. Upon questioning a relative who had recently returned from Vietnam about the situation, I was told that the brothers were "more united against the honkies than against the VC." Discord is certainly at its highest point in American military history. A large portion of this discord is the result of opposition to the Vietnam War. But an equal portion is being produced by growing pride and bitterness among black soldiers.

In the midst of the turmoil and confusion of a corrupt society, the black youth must make decisions about the direction that he must take. He is confronted with three choices: he may attempt to assimilate into the racist society; he may seek revolutionary change; or finally, he may seek independence of white America.

Assimilation has historically been a failure. It is obvious that white society is only willing to absorb a minute number of blacks, and commonly these lose all identity. Closely associated with assimilation is the belief that the American democracy will correct past evils. This is very debatable. Some might point out how black people have advanced since slavery. I would answer this by noting that we were at the bottom then, and we're at the bottom now. At any rate, let us assume that the American democracy will correct its own evils. Still one point is undebatable: the process is extremely slow and I question whether black people are willing to wait.

The popular and contemporary approach to the problems of black people is revolutionary change, as expressed by the Black Panther Party. Involved in this approach is the belief that fascist America can be defeated by a people's army composed of poor and working-class people. I have one grave reservation: the white working classes have proven themselves as racist and pro–fascist United States as any segment of American society. They demonstrated this dramatically in Pittsburgh and Chicago, where white workers marched against blacks trying to obtain more jobs in the building trades. One common argument alleges that unions are part of the fascist Establishment and hence not really controlled by the workers, thus making the problem one of class rather than race. However, the experience of most people I know has been based on race not class.

Our last choice appears to offer the most hope. What is meant by independence? I would not consider liberated territory at this point. First, I would say we must have mental freedom. This means that we would no longer depend on our enemy for ideas, information and a sense of ourselves. This mental freedom would direct us to look toward Africa and our black brothers for our needs, be they mental or physical. Involved in this independence is the realization that we must control our own educational system to insure our freedom.

Mental and educational freedom is the origin of all economic and political self-reliance. It is necessary for this process to take place before any meaningful decision about going back to Africa or separating ourselves from whites or even integrating into America can be made. So we, black youth, should begin freeing our minds and educating ourselves to form a new world liberated of the falsehoods that have oppressed our people for so many centuries.

David Friedman

David Friedman graduated Phi Beta Kappa from Harvard in 1965, received a masters degree in physics from the University of Chicago in 1967 and is now finishing his doctorate in theoretical physics. While at Harvard, he won a prize for lyric poetry, founded the Harvard Society of Individualists and was Associate Editor of the *Harvard Conservative*. For the past two years he has written a regular libertarian column in *The New Guard*, the official magazine of the Young Americans for Freedom, under the running head of "The Radical."

The newspapers, as usual, have missed the boat. There is a New Politics, but Eugene McCarthy never heard of it. It is spreading like wildfire among the young political activists of the right, and has a solid toehold among their opposite numbers on the left. In another two years, we will control or make obsolete the right's major youth group, Young Americans for Freedom. Our first candidate may be Tim Leary.

We call ourselves libertarians; some of us call ourselves libertarian anarchists. Our ideology is capitalism, carried to its logical ends.

We believe in a totally free society in which every man can think, say and smoke what he likes, do business with anyone on any mutually agreeable terms and sleep with anyone willing to sleep with him. We believe in such a society, and we know how to make it work.

We believe that the only way in which white men can interact freely in a free society is through the institution of private property—that absolute property rights are a necessary condition for freedom. It is this that makes us unpopular with the socialist ideologues who dominate the left.

In any society there are property rights, because in any society there are things that several people wish to use and only one can. We cannot all simultaneously drive the same car to our different homes. There must be some rules determining how such scarce resources are to be used. Under the system of private property, each such object belongs to some one person who has the absolute right to decide on its use. Private property is the ultimate form of decentralization. Under other institutions, the decision is made by some political body.

Socialists object that under a system of private property it is possible for a man to starve. They forget that property always exists, and that only the state can control all property, and so have the power to impose starvation on its enemies—a fact attested to by thousands of live American communists and millions of dead Russian kulaks. A government that can give food to one man can take it from another.

When property is held by political institutions, it is used to impose the ends of those controlling institutions on everyone. When property is held privately, it is used by each individual, freely cooperating with others, to serve his own ends.

Consider, as a concrete example, the difference between newspapers and magazines on the one hand, and radio and TV on the other.

Printed media, which require for their production only private resources, range from the *Chicago Tribune* to the *Berkeley Barb*, from *Time* to *The Realist*. As long as some tiny minority likes a magazine, that magazine can survive (although the government postal monopoly may not deliver it).

There is no radio station in the country on which the classified pages of the *Barb* could be read aloud. There is no TV station that would broadcast the cartoons from one issue of *The Realist*. Radio and TV operate on public property.

The government owns the air waves. It permits the broadcasters to use them as long as their programming is "in the public interest"—as judged by the government. The majority can, and frequently does, keep the minority from presenting its views. The most famous example was the BBC's refusal, during the late thirties, to allow Winston Churchill on the air. They believed that the propagation of his alarmist view of Germany was not "in the national interest."

The problem arises from government power. The solution is to divide the power and transfer it to private hands—to propertize it. Auction off the airwaves, frequency by frequency, to the highest bidders. Since supply greatly exceeds present demand, the price will be low. If the owner of one frequency doesn't like a show's politics, the producer of the show will find another who does, or who doesn't care about politics as long as he is paid on time.

Some people will be offended by what they hear on the station owned by the *Berkeley Barb*. The same people are offended by the knowledge that someone somewhere is smoking pot, or engaging in premarital sex. Their paradigm is the lady who complained to the police that a man three blocks away undressed without drawing his blinds. She could see him clearly—through her telescope.

This example of the libertarian approach may explain why we are unpopular with that large segment of conservative opinion that concerns itself with the moral breakdown of society, seeing behind every topless dancer the decline and fall of the Roman Empire.

But what, the liberal will ask, of the necessity to use government to solve the problems of society—the problems of poverty, hunger, population, pollution?

Several years ago a friend of mine attended a meeting where Senator Keating gave a speech about the necessity of government action to encourage the use of birth control. Afterwards, my friend asked him whether the government might begin by repealing the laws that make it illegal to advertise methods of birth control in the public press. No, he replied, that would be too radical a solution.

The liberals can start worrying about using government to prevent hunger after they have abolished the agriculture program that wastes some $10 billion a year trying to make food more expensive. They can talk about providing decent housing for the poor after they have abolished their urban renewal program, whose main function is replacing blacks with grass, and after they have done away with the building codes that are used by the building trades unions to make technological innovation illegal and thus force builders to build badly and expensively. They can use government to solve the pollution problem when government ceases to be the nation's number one polluter, and when the government of the state of Illinois ceases to require that its buildings be heated only with high-sulfur coal, an Illinois product.

Government isn't the solution, it's the problem.

The same applies to the problems of minorities. The main reason why blacks, alone among minorities, have remained in the ghetto has nothing to do with racial differences, genetic or cultural. The earlier waves of immigrants, including blacks who came North and prospered before and after the Civil War, had the good fortune to arrive in a society of almost unrestricted laissez-faire. Blacks coming North in recent decades have faced a much less open and flexible society. Massive governmental intervention, introduced supposedly for the protection of the weak, had, and has, as its actual function the protection of the status quo. Fifty or a hundred years ago, established workers had no way to protect themselves against the competition of immigrants, just as established firms, contrary to popular belief, had no way to keep new firms from competing with them (Standard Oil's share of the market, for example, declined slowly but steadily for thirty years prior to the time it was broken up). That problem has since been solved. Our society is now equipped with a hundred statist devices—from craft unions to minimum wage laws, from licensing of restaurants to licensing of plumbers—by which the ins can and do protect themselves against the outs.

Examples of how regulation protects regulated industries are legion. Before the creation of the Interstate Commerce Commission (ICC), railroads running between the same cities by different routes had to charge competitive rates on the "long haul," but charged high rates for the "short haul" between intermediate cities, where each railroad had a monopoly. The ICC was created and rectified this injustice by raising the long-haul rates. Currently, the Civil Aeronautics Board (CAB) sets fares for interstate airlines. PSA, a California intrastate airline, and so outside the CAB's jurisdiction, has driven the fare between San Francisco and Los Angeles down to about half the fare on comparable interstate routes. Since the CAB was created, to "protect" passengers from the dangers of low fares, no major interstate airline has been founded.

Another area of concern to libertarians is education. The present school system is a statist monster, built on the premise that the government knows what children should be taught and should teach it to them, whether they like it or not. As a first step, we should abolish compulsory attendance laws. A school that cannot keep its pupils without help from the police is a custodial institution, a jail (and youth is not a crime.) As another step, we should end the government monopoly of schooling by making the money now used to subsidize the public schools equally available to parents who choose to send their children to private schools. That would create a market for inexpensive, privately run schools, which would provide a better education than the public schools at a comparable cost.

Our position on foreign policy is summarized by a remark attributed to Ronald Hamoway: "I am not a pacifist. I am only opposed, in principle, to communist wars. A communist war is any war fought between governments."

We are anticommunist. We are more anticommunist than the conservatives, for we include in our anticommunism opposition to communist institutions in our midst, such as the selective service system. We trust the government to protect us little more than we trust it to feed us, and so we view with some suspicion the massive and bloody foreign interventions that it justifies as a necessary part of our defense. We are the only people in America who will ever admit to being isolationists.

We are isolationist only militarily. In other respects we are internationalist—in our fashion. The liberal dreams of destroying the power of the nation state and replacing it with the power of the international state. We dream of destroying the power of all states. The liberal dreams of the day when the UN will be as powerful as the federal government. We dream of the day when all governments will be as impotent as the UN.

Our utopia (every movement has one) is a less orderly place than the utopias of conservatives, liberals or socialists. Somewhere in it there is a socialist community, somewhere a workers' cooperative, somewhere, perhaps, a village theocracy. If any group of people wish to associate with each other on such terms, that is their business, provided only that they do not force the rest of us to be part of their system. In a socialist society all resources come from the common store; if I disapprove of what you are doing, I must try to stop you from wasting the society's wealth. In our society you are directing your resources to your ends, and I am directing my resources to mine.

Somewhere, in our utopia, there may be a man who is ignorant or poor; somewhere a man may corrupt another's mind with lies or destroy his own body with drugs. We do not pretend that any society, least of all a free society, can be safe.

If, as some on the left expect, automation does usher in a period of unimaginable plenty, then food will be provided free in our utopia, exactly as most water is provided free today, because charging for it is more trouble than it is worth. If, as some expect, pollution increases until air and water are no longer free goods, then the society will evolve institutions to propertize air and water and impose costs upon those who damage them.

We cannot predict the details of a free society. We cannot predict the actions of free men voluntarily associating for the achievement of their individual ends. We can predict that such a society will work, for we have seen it work again and again in those areas of human life where men have been allowed to be free. We do not accept slavery as a necessary part of the human condition.

The conservative says that we are immoral, for we have imagined a society with no protection against those who would corrupt it. The liberal says we are heartless, for we have imagined a society with no authority to force men to do good.

"Puritanism—The haunting fear that someone, somewhere, is happy."
—H. L. Mencken, *Sententiae*

"If I knew for a certainty that a man was coming to my house with the conscious design of doing me good, I should run for my life."
—Henry David Thoreau, *Walden*

"No promises, you note, are made to the turned-on young who have everything they need if only they were left alone."
—Timothy Leary, talking about his 1970 California gubernatorial campaign

Laissez-faire.

Leon Gussow

A twenty-four-year-old med school dropout, Leon
Gussow did receive his B.A. from Cornell and has
written for *Rat*, the weekly underground newspaper. As
for the future, he says, "I might keep writing, might
go back to school, might just freak out. . . ."

✢✢✢✢✢✢✢✢✢✢✢✢✢✢✢✢✢✢✢✢✢✢✢✢✢✢✢✢✢✢✢✢✢✢✢✢✢✢

One hundred and one things the government should
not do:

1. Keep armed forces in Vietnam.
2. Put Dr. Spock in jail.
3. Put Huey Newton in jail.
4. Put Eldridge Cleaver in jail.
5. Put me in jail.
6. Put anyone in jail.
7. Draft young men to fight in wars they don't support.
8. Draft young men to fight in wars they do support.
9. Institute an army of professional mercenaries (read: blacks and other minority groups).
10. Allow Walt Disney Productions, Inc., to rape our American landscape.
11. Maintain job corps programs that prepare young men for jobs no one else wants.
12. Maintain job corps programs that prepare young men for jobs that don't exist.
13. Maintain job corps programs that prepare young men for jobs they don't want.
14. Maintain job corps programs that prepare young men for service in the armed forces.
15. Keep armed forces in Thailand.

16. Classify documents "top secret" solely to keep them from its own citizens.

17. Negotiate cost-plus contracts with the aerospace industry, by which companies are reimbursed for expenses over their original bids (thus encouraging inefficiency, waste and fraud).

18. Subsidize the oil industry by shielding the domestic market from low-cost foreign competition, thus doubling the price of oil to the American consumer.

19. Subsidize the automobile and highway-building industries by means of the gasoline tax.

20. Help the United States cattle industry maintain artificially inflated prices by banning Argentine meat from the country.

21. Spend billions on obsolete defense systems that are never put into operation and are ultimately abandoned.

22. Spend even more billions for defense systems that eventually *are* put into operation.

23. Prosecute draft-card burners.

24. Prosecute draft-board burners.

25. Keep armed forces in Korea.

26. Staff the Defense Department with men who are about to become executives of companies holding defense contracts.

27. Refuse to hire homosexuals for civil service positions.

28. Subsidize the automobile industry by building useless and obsolete highways like the Long Island Expressway.

29. Destroy what little remains of Indian culture by taking Indian children from their homes and sending them to boarding schools for "education" or "job training."

30. Continue to finance social security through pay-

roll deductions rather than through income taxes.

31. Keep armed forces in Japan.

32. Jail draft resisters who return from exile in Canada or Sweden.

33. Jail the Black Panthers who return from exile in Cuba.

34. Continue the national campaign to wipe out the Black Panther Party.

35. Subsidize oil milliionaires through such tax dodges as depletion allowances (which exempt 22 percent of income from oil wells from taxation) and intangible drilling expense deductions.

36. Allow a privileged few Americans (seventy of them in 1969) to make unlimited tax-deductible contributions to charity.

37. Allow earnings from state and local bonds to be immune from taxation.

38. Allow $13 billion in "capital gains" income to be free from taxation each year.

39. Allow Congressmen to regulate companies and financial institutions in which they have a personal interest.

40. Keep armed forces in the Philippines.

41. Waste billions on a manned moon-exploration program.

42. Waste more billions on a program to land a man on Mars.

43. Refuse to set up adequate safety standards to protect miners.

44. Act as a censor on what can and cannot be sent through the mails.

45. Act as a censor on what can and cannot be said on radio and television.

46. Develop advanced weapons systems for the control of its own population during domestic riots.

47. Threaten to cut off federal aid to college students

as a means of controlling their political behavior.

48. Maintain "detention camps" for the mass imprisonment of demonstrators, protestors and radicals.

49. Keep armed forces in Greece.

50. Allow the reactionary American Medical Association to determine the nation's health policies and activities.

51. Maintain a tax structure that is predominantly based on the taxation of lower- and middle-class salaries rather than the taxation of upper-class accumulated wealth.

52. Quarantine Cuba.

53. Reimburse defense industries for rent they pay on their plants.

54. Permit defense contractors to retain exclusive patents on the by-products of research paid for by public taxes.

55. Arbitrarily suppress reports by its own committees, such as the four-man study of the Bay of Pigs fiasco.

56. Keep armed forces in Turkey.

57. Take part in and profit from the slaughter of seals in the Bering Sea Islands.

58. Use supposed "antipoverty" programs to maximize the profits of big business in poor communities while doing nothing to aid the people of those communities.

59. Use the Defense Department for "solving" social problems.

60. Evict people from their homes for dubious "urban renewal" programs.

61. Evict people from their homes to build sterile centers of bourgeois "culture."

62. Rob Latin America of its natural resources, paying only a fraction of their value.

63. Grant loans to Latin American countries (through the Export-Import Bank, the International Monetary Fund and such) that serve not to help the countries achieve badly needed diversification of their economies, but merely to make them financially dependent on the United States.

64. Use multinational organizations (OAS, SEATO, ets.) as fronts for American intervention into the affairs of foreign countries.

65. Institute or continue spurious pseudoaltruistic programs like the Alliance for Progress to neutralize the desire of the Latin American people for real social and political reform.

66. Use indictments for "conspiracy" as a political weapon.

67. Employ military spending power to negate the effects of consumer boycotts (as in the case of the national boycott in support of the California grape workers' strike).

68. Keep armed forces in Germany.

69. Napalm marijuana fields in Mexico.

70. Allow prison inmates to be used as guinea pigs in unregulated and unethical medical experiments.

71. Allow drugs to be put on the market after only hasty and superficial testing and evaluation.

72. Allow pharmaceutical companies to have evaluative testing of their products done by their own paid hirelings.

73. Ship deadly nerve gas through populated areas.

74. Test chemical and biological weapons in the open air.

75. Allow the legislative functions of Congress to become a mask for political persecution and harassment (through "investigations" of SDS, campus activists, etc.).

76. Negotiate and sign secret agreements with foreign countries.
77. Turn over control of American troops to foreign governments.
78. Store chemical and biological weapons on foreign soil.
79. Store chemical and biological weapons on American soil.
80. Keep armed forces in Italy.
81. Give Senator Eastland up to $129,997 a year for *not* growing cotton.
82. Sell arms to Israel.
83. Sell arms to Jordan.
84. Prohibit the use of marijuana.
85. Prohibit the use of LSD.
86. Prohibit the use of mescaline.
87. Prohibit the use of peyote.
88. Keep armed forces in Cuba.
89. Allow private industry to ruin our air and water.
90. Support black capitalism.
91. Support white capitalism.
92. Collect money.
93. Spend money.
94. Print money.
95. Legislate morality.
96. Legislate immorality.
97. Enforce laws.
98. Make laws.
99. Repress.
100. Oppress.
101. Exist.

José Angel Gutierrez

Founder and presently project director in southwest
Texas for the Winter Garden Project, José Angel
Gutierrez is twenty-four, married to Luz Bazan and
the father of one son, Adrian. Mr. Gutierrez has at-
tended the University of Texas, Colorado State College,
Trinity University and Arizona State, also lecturing at
Texas A. and I. and Michigan State. Born in Crystal
City, he is a "child of the political revolution" that
began there in 1963, with marches and school walk-
outs spreading to Austin and Del Rio. "Various po-
litical pimps have been after our organization with
Congressional investigations, but they've never been
effective except in cutting funds from the gutless Ford
Foundation."

Texas is part of the South! The same cruel and
vicious disregard for human life exists in all of Texas
as does in all the other Southern states. The only difference is in the color of the people oppressed. We are
not black, nor are we white. We are brown. We are
Chicanos. The others are gringos. Our gringos are no
different from the Selma cracker, the Newark honky
or the Nashville redneck. Our gringos are equally
bigoted, un-American, racist and animalistic.

We call them gringos just like our forefathers did
and for the very same reasons. A gringo to us is a foreigner, a thief, an exploiter, and usually from North
America. These barbarians came from the North into
our lands and through fraud and murder stole our
property and our right to full human development. We
have been made colonial subjects. South Texas is comparable to Haiti and the Dominican Republic.

La raza is wealthless. We have no land, no mineral rights, no money, and even less prospects of ever acquiring any. *La raza* is crippled and infirm. Over a third of our people are illiterate, half live in poverty and all of us have been victims of cultural genocide. Through the years the gringo's racism and basic hatred for life has been forced upon us. The gringo cannot tolerate innocence or sanity. He must destroy and cripple in order to bring others to his level of animalism. His lies of white supremacy have been beaten into our heads. His racism has been seared into our personalities. Only a gringo could and would kill and steal under the slogan of Manifest Destiny. Only a gringo would prohibit the speaking of our language, Spanish, claiming it to be a subversive act and basically un-American. Only a gringo would laugh at our food and music and yet stuff himself on *tacos* while listening to the Tijuana Brass. We have endured this and much more, but the scars of exploitation, so readily discernible, are painful reminders that we must rid ourselves of these gringos if we are to survive as a family of *Mexicanos*.

Our parents have been made weak. Through the years they have learned to accept humiliation and reproach. They bitterly got accustomed to letting the gringo have his way. Consequently, our organizations have been weak and ineffective. They have relied too heavily on the traditional approach toward problem-solving—petitions, resolutions, conventions and the like. Every effort was nonviolent and very low key. Only recently have a few groups learned to confront the powers that be and demand redress. Protest in the streets has been used effectively. Now our leaders go to the people with plans for action. And there is a unity among our leaders and organizations that had been lacking for so long.

It used to be that soon after a leader emerged the

Establishment would co-opt him for their purposes. Many of our leaders in business, politics and social circles were representatives *to* the Mexican-American community rather than leaders *from* the community. But old leadership styles and traditional organizations gave way to new Chicano leaders and new organizations. These new movers are cramped in their efforts due to the lack of available resources. The foundations, afraid of Congress, are not funding effective programs for community action and voter registration. There are few meaningful federal programs, and those few that are initiated seldom get refunded after the first year. There is no money available for such things as leadership training and the acquiring of expertise in housing and economic development. The situation is critical behind the cactus curtain.

All too often governmental agencies, foundations and business interests argue that the geographic location of the South and the Southwest doesn't lend itself to development and promotion. That there are few metropolitan areas in these regions is another excuse for inaction. And of course there is no "black problem" in Texas. The latter statement reflects the thinking of many policy makers and program planners. It seems that our minority is to be the last in the pecking order of priorities. We have become an invisible minority, not of our own choosing, but because we have been made silent. The news media have never reported important events in our communities as frequently as they occur, not to mention the extent of their coverage when it does exist. Journalists, unfamiliar with our culture and language, make grave errors of perception. Many stereotypes and generalizations are made that can be neither rationalized nor justified, because they are not made out of ignorance but stupidity.

The gravest sin to date committed by the media,

social scientists, businessmen and government agents is
the creation of the myth that *la raza* is silent, permissive and without protest. We have never been silent,
permissive or without protest. For example, between
the Nueces River and the Rio Grande, bands of Mexican guerillas operated until 1910 seeking the overthrow of the government. In the thirties and forties
there were many labor strikes and labor movements by
Mexican Americans throughout the Southwest. The
forties and the fifties saw the formation of mass membership organizations, such as the GI Forum and the
League of United Latin American Councils. Numerous
school segregation cases were fought during the post-
World War II period in such Texas towns as Del Rio,
San Antonio and Crystal City. There were school walkouts and demonstrations in San Antonio in the thirties
and forties led by Eluterio Escobar, who is still alive
and well in the *barrio* where he was born.

The sixties saw the formation of political organiza-
tions and a formidable entry into Presidential politics.
The Viva Kennedy Clubs evolved into the Political
Association of Spanish-Speaking Organizations (PASO).
Various chapters sprung up throughout the south Texas
area and began registering voters and fielding candi-
dates in the rural areas. Victories were recorded in
Crystal City, Mathis and New Braunfels, Texas, and
Seguin and Pasadena, California, and a host of other
places in New Mexico and Arizona.

Youth groups began forming in the late sixties, such
as the United Mexican American Students and the
Brown Berets (California), Mexican American Youth
Organization (Texas), the Crusade for Justice (Colorado), and the Mexican American Student Organization (Arizona). Also in the sixties the Alianza Federal
de Mercedes led a powerful fight for the return of
stolen land grants in New Mexico. There have been

riots in Denver, Los Angeles and Kalamazoo this past year. Farm workers have organized and gone on strike in Delano, Wautoma, Wisconsin, the Rio Grande Valley and Ohio. There have been no less than eight school walkouts this past year in south Texas. Palm Sunday, 1969, saw over three thousand Chicanos marching in the streets of Del Rio, Texas, to protest the termination of the VISTA Minority Mobilization project in that county.

Yet our efforts have gone unnoticed and unheeded. Must we resort to violence in order to gain national publicity? Is it not enough to march hundreds of miles in protest? Or to have hundreds of students arrested, expelled, suspended and jailed for protesting the denial of their right to self-expression, the right to speak Spanish? Aren't the statistics found in numerous studies describing our wretched social condition enough to prick the conscience of this country?

Examining the experience of the late Dr. Martin Luther King, it is apparent that his victories came during times of violence. A handful of black militants can push this country into a panic through rough talk and ominous warnings. Must we also yell and riot in order to get on the list of priorities? Are we to believe that it takes one riot to get a federal grant, one death to produce a Department of Justice investigation and one shooting to gain a minute of time on Walter Cronkite? There seems to be no other alternative. For example, a major national magazine recently refused to publicize a school demonstration in which 116 students were jailed simply because there had been no confrontation between the Texas Rangers and the demonstrators. Their formula of two bashed heads for one inch of column is indicative of the madness inherent in this society—a madness that revels in violence and danger.

Due to our reluctance to engage in acts of violence,

the social scientists will no doubt continue to blame our innate cultural characteristics for our failure to achieve "upward mobility." The President will hold yet another White House conference on the problems of the Mexican Americans, and the media will continue to ignore our battle for human dignity, all the while hiding behind their own shortcomings. Nobody seems to care about our burden of poverty, injustice, unequal opportunity, illness and human degradation. Nobody cares what the gringo does to *la raza.*

Our parents are tired and tried. They have slowly given up the struggle. More affluent Mexican Americans find it easier to work with the gringos rather than resist the injustices. So the fight for liberation falls on the youth. And the fight must be successful, for the whole of our existence depends on this struggle. Our survival is at stake.

In 1960 more than 50 percent of all Mexican-American families in Texas had annual incomes below $3,000. In fact, 30 percent of all families with Spanish surnames had incomes of less than $2,000! *La raza* has a median education of 6.1 years as compared to 11.5 for whites and 8.1 for Negroes. In Zavala county the median education for Chicanos in 1950 was 1.8 years; in 1960 it was 2.3 years. An increase of half a grade level in ten years is not progress! Adding to the problem of low incomes and illiteracy is our median family size—4.6 persons. Over 46 percent of all our people live in overcrowded housing and 12 percent live in dilapidated housing. Our median income in 1960 was $2,914 and our per capita income was $629!

In spite of these statistics our people do not lose hope. But our faith in democracy has long been lost. There are many reasons. Proportionally, our young men die in Vietnam at a higher rate than any other minority group. We continue to eke out a living at farm labor while white Americans have strawberries on their Kel logs, lettuce in their salads and onions on their hamburgers. We have been forced to laugh at poverty. We must do everything possible for survival, using anything at hand to enjoy our present empty life. (As an example, in Texas nine out of ten families living in poverty receive no assistance from federal food programs.)

The American Dream is but an empty slogan. The only realities in America today are its cruelty and hatred for anybody off-white. Yet our ethnic group is basically devoid of racism and reaction. Presently white America is concerned that Martin Luther King be made a saint. For years we have revered St. Martin de Porres, a black man. For years our people have been neither reactionary nor radical. When our lands in *Aztlan* (the Southwest to you) were made United States government property, our people remained devout, culturally conservative and proud, and loyal to the new government. We have endured all that has been meted out to us in the hope that soon America would stop treating us like bastard children. We had hoped that we would be made a part of America with all the rights and privileges other Americans enjoy. But that was a foolish dream because today America continues to exact from us more than we are able to give.

We cannot be expected to identify with the Pilgrims and Jamestown when our forefathers were Spaniards and *Aztecas* and our settlements were *San Augustine, Florida, Sante Fe, Neuvo Mexico,* and *San Antonio, Tejas.* Our war hero is Cleto Rodriguez of *San Marcos, Tejas,* not Audie Murphy. We cannot accept the theme of law and order because that gives license to the infamous Texas Rangers for further cruelty and terror. We cannot believe that the first steps on the moon were for the good of mankind because we have never been included in the definition of the word. Nor can we understand how the government so readily subsidizes the businessmen of agriculture and the oil barons while cutting expenditures for the poverty-shackled.

It is clear to us, the young Mexican Americans, that we must disturb America into action. The government must be made more responsible to our needs. Business and industry must be made to relocate in the Southwest, and not in Mexico or abroad. The news media must be made to relate the problems and struggles of *la raza*. Private money must be made available for education, housing, economic development and health services. The land in the Southwest must be redistributed to give the poor a much larger share. The oil industry must be made to return some profits to be used for employment-training programs and for low-interest loans for the poor. In short, white Americans must quickly make a serious commitment to our well-being, for if we are pushed further down on the scale of human worth, it is a fact that we will resist with all effort. We cannot be expected to live in museums or on reservations to serve as artifacts of the twentieth century.

If need be we will follow the sage advice of our hero Emiliano Zapata:

> *Es mejor morir de pies que vivir de rodillas.*
> (It is better to die on your feet than to live on your knees.)

Clifton Hill

A former Golden Glove champion and Baptist minister, Clifton Hill is now a leader of the Creek Centralization Committee of the back-country Creek bands in Oklahoma.

✦✦✦

I, Clifton Hill, am officiating chairman of the Traditional Indians of the Creek Tribes, consisting of the Hitchitas, Notchas, Cowarsatas, Alabamas, Yutchis and Seminoles of Oklahoma. I am also a standing member of the National Traditional Movement of United States, Canada and Mexico.

When I was a little boy in the country I saw a snake trying to swallow a frog. The frog cried out as the snake slowly swallowed it. We Indians are in the wheel of progress, swallowed up as the times are changing. We are also in great turmoil, for the corruption and injustice in the Bureau of Indian Affairs is swallowing us up slowly as the snake swallowed the frog. But there was a solution: the frog swallowed air, became too big for the snake to digest and escaped. In the same sense, there is a solution for our Indian problem. We traditionals are working hard toward that aim and slowly we are coming to a better understanding through unity for a noble purpose.

One of our greatest chiefs was known as Crazy Snake. Early one morning he saw a mass of soldiers surrounding him and his braves. So he said, "This is a good day to die for my people," and he fought to the last drop of his blood. I have the same faith. As long as warm blood flows in my veins through the blessing of our Creator, I will stand and fight for my people.

This then is a submittal of proposals voiced in general by the Traditional Indians of the Creek Nation in the State of Oklahoma. Our aim is to stand on American principles, to promote the general welfare of the American Indians and to protect our inherited rights as provided for by laws and treaties. We submit these demands to those who have the responsibility to enforce the law and we request a sincere negotiation to insure that justice be restored after over 150 years of "Indian Problems."

1. We request an amendment to Executive Order 10250 of April 26, 1906, which stipulates that the President shall appoint our leaders. We are dissatisfied and do not want Presidential appointment of our alleged leaders. According to our constitutional rights, we are entitled to participate in local, state and national elections. But these rights are denied to the Indian, for under executive order we are prohibited from electing our chief and council members. With the present widespread antidiscrimination sentiment and concern for allowing every citizen to exercise his rights, we too want to elect our representatives the American way: by popular vote in a free nation.

2. We request an immediate investigation of the handling of our tribal trust fund, our resources and our government funds. Without the consent of the tribes, committees of non-Indians and the Bureau of Indian Affairs have continually prorated funds out of our hands by programming the money for tourist attractions, so-called cultural centers, industrial sites, etc. Somehow the biggest profits from these programs always go to outsiders, while the Indian Fund gets only a drop in the bucket. This is known as "helping the Indians," but we call it maladministration. Surveys

made from 1900 to 1930 reported governmental misuse of tribal trust funds without our consent or compensation, and even today this unwise and unfair expenditure of tribal monies continues.

3. We request compensation for the forced movements of our tribes in 1932 and 1936. These movements inflicted great suffering, mistreatment, death and humiliation. The survivors were left in great confusion, robbed of their once-proud dignity, heritage and traditions. This was genocide.

4. We request that the authorities honor our ancestral fishing and hunting rights as ratified by treaty with the United States government. Fishing and hunting continue to provide our livelihood and principle means of support. Despite all the money in the Bureau of Indian Affairs, the Indian tribes across the United States are in a desperate economic condition. Consequently, the Indian still depends on fishing and hunting for survival. He never kills wild game for sport, as the white man does. The Indian fishes and hunts for food to feed his family. So these fishing and hunting treaties must be honored.

5. We request immediate cessation of various states' infringement on the treaty rights of the Indian tribes. Many states are violating treaties, causing violent harassment and brutality for Indians who are trying to uphold their rights. This persecution is causing Indians to bitterly retaliate against these calamities.

One such case is the famous Battle of the Big Bend. In 1966 the Pit River Indians blockaded a road that cut through the Rancheria Indian Reservation Village. This road was used for heavy trucking by the big logging companies of the Pacific Northwest. The protest began against the trucks speeding through the village, creating clouds of dust in the summer and rivers of mud in the winter, endangering the health of the villagers and the lives of their children. Deputy Sheriff Treve Merrifield and U.S. Forest Service official Wesley Lewis threatened the protestors with arrest and imprisonment, but the Indians continued to block the road. Then Shasta County Superior Court Judge Richard B. Eaton stepped in and issued a temporary restraining order against the Indians, but the blockade continued. Next five sheriffs raided the blockade, subduing and handcuffing Willard Rhoads, while three other deputy sheriffs captured Kenneth Sisk, firing guns at the people and breaking Grandma Sisk's arm. Meanwhile four other deputies under the personal direction of Sheriff John Balma captured Jack Potter and hauled him off to jail with the others. But volunteer attorney Jack Halpin defended these men successfully, they were soon released and the blockade continued. Finally the area director of the Bureau of Indian Affairs threatened federal court action, but the Indians ran him off their land. They stood fast, the trucking was diverted and a major victory against all these big bureaucracies was won.

Another case was the 1965 incident at Frank's Landing on the Nisqually River at Nisqually, Washington. For generations the Indians have fished on this river, but beginning a few years back, Indian men, women and children were arrested, mistreated, jailed and fined by state officials whenever they attempted to exercise these ancient rights. Finally the case was tried in the United States Circuit Court of Appeals before Judge Franklin K. Thorpe, and with the help of Alvin Ziontz, an attorney from Seattle, the Indians won the case.

Still another incident was the Case of the Deer

Slayer. John Chewie, a young full-blooded Indian, killed a deer to feed his hungry family on the Kenwood Indian Reservation in the region of Woodland, which is held in trust by the United States government for the Cherokee tribe. Because Chewie didn't have a license, he was arrested and put in jail by the Oklahoma State Department of Wildlife. But this caused a tremendous disturbance among the tribes in Oklahoma, and once again the case was decided in their favor—a great victory.

6. We are very much opposed to Omnibus Bill H.R. 10560, known as the Termination Bill. If this piece of legislation is passed, the American Indian, true native of this great nation, will be victim of further treachery. The passage of this bill would disregard the most binding promises, disenfranchising the Indian from traditional federal protection and ignoring centuries of solemn treaties.

7. We request that the United States settle our claim growing out of the Fort Jackson Treaty of 1814, under which the government acquired a large amount of land belonging to the Creek Nation without any payment. We think a purchase price of $29 million for this land, plus a 4 percent interest rate for the years 1814 to 1970, is just. There are many such claims remaining unsettled and we request that each of them be resolved with justice for the Indian tribes.

The Bureau of Indian Affairs has continually misrepresented my people and has proposed legislation detrimental to the Indian and without the consent of the tribes themselves. The present system of a Bureau of Indian Affairs plus Presidentially appointed leaders ignores the voice and true wishes of the Indian, who is denied his rights and knows little of how his affairs are being managed. This situation is causing great dissension in the four corners of our great nation. The American Indian does not want violence, but he does want justice, peace and freedom. He wants the right to voice his opinion and participate in his own tribal affairs.

Many of our braves have fought on distant battlefields, dying to defend peace and freedom for their homeland. But when they return, they are denied the very rights they have fought for.

Mr. President of the United States, representative of all the people, you promised us justice and a new policy for peace and progress abroad and at home. Will you hear the cry of the American Indian, the true native of this land, the real forgotten American?

In the year 1492, when the white man first set foot on the red man's soil, the Indian received this foreigner royally and supported him in the struggle for justice, freedom and liberty. But the white man became a savage, slaughtering peaceable Indians and taking away their land through fraudulence and force. This injustice has been constantly repeated throughout the history of the United States. The American Indian has been misrepresented, misunderstood and denied his rights for centuries, right up to and including today. We are much concerned over the vital problems confronting the Indian now and request that you consider the numerous cases of Indian rights that are continuously being denied. We insist that you take action on these cases and help us insure the recognition of treaties and rights.

The American Indian has the highest rate of poverty, the worst educational opportunities, the highest rate of unemployment, the lowest average income, the poorest health facilities, the highest death rate . . . there is much more to tell, but we will be brief, hoping you will understand our grievances and objectives. The fact is, the needs, welfare and interests of the tribes are not being served, and this is demoralizing the Indian's spirit and life, causing great disillusion in our people. We have great hopes that you will give us a satisfactory reply to our needs, that the best interests of all can be served.

Respectfully submitted by the Traditional Indians of the Creek Tribes, consisting of Hitchitas, Notchas, Cowarsatas, Alabamas, Yutchis and Seminoles in the State of Oklahoma.

Kasoundra Kasoundra

A twenty-four-year-old artist living on New York's Lower East Side, Kasoundra Kasoundra "believes in nothing and everything. And when I grow up I want to be a saint." A sometime astrologer and reader of Tarot cards, she has appeared on the *Merv Griffin Show* and in the movie *Alice's Restaurant*.

❧❧❧❧❧❧❧❧❧❧❧❧❧❧❧❧❧❧❧❧❧❧❧❧❧❧❧❧❧❧❧

A Declaration of Indigestion

When, in the course of human events, it becomes necessary for one people to dissolve the political bands which have connected them with one another, and to assume, among the powers of the earth, the separate and equal station to which the laws of nature and of nature's God entitle them, a decent respect to the opinions of mankind requires that they should declare the causes which impel them to the separation.

THE PRESIDENT HAS REFUSED HIS ASSENT TO LAWS THE MOST WHOLESOME AND NECESSARY FOR THE PUBLIC GOOD.

Bakers have refused to assert their loaves, the most wholesome for the public good, they grow stale and white in air. Why should any man go hungry? Proclaim to this bakeman that all mouths shall be full, that bread should be broken at every table. Why should any man go hungry?

HE HAS FORBIDDEN HIS GOVERNORS TO PASS LAWS OF IMMEDIATE AND PRESSING IMPORTANCE, UNLESS SUSPENDED IN THEIR OPERATION TILL HIS ASSENT SHOULD BE OBTAINED; AND WHEN SO SUSPENDED, HE HAS UTTERLY NEGLECTED TO ATTEND TO THEM.

Cooks refuse laws of immediate importance. Their recipes are in operation, but they neglect the ingredients. They have also neglected the kitchens. There is no one to attend to them.

Spring proclaims the lands for growing. Youthful growing in minds and harvest. Let the reaper gather the old way with the new shafts and tend them with a grain of thought.

HE HAS CALLED TOGETHER LEGISLATIVE BODIES AT PLACES UNUSUAL, UNCOMFORTABLE, AND DISTANT FROM THE DEPOSITORY OF THEIR PUBLIC HAPPENING, FOR THE SOLE PURPOSE OF FATIGUING THEM INTO COMPLIANCE WITH HIS MEASURES.

We have been too long without a public hearth and our union suffers. We are fatigued with complying.

In bars our union is dissolved repeatedly, also much manly firmness by the intoxications on the rights of the gentleman. There is too much luxury for those who are easy.

HE HAS ERECTED A MULTITUDE OF NEW OFFICES, AND SENT HITHER SWARMS OF OFFICERS TO HARASS OUR PEOPLE, AND EAT OUT THEIR SUBSTANCE.

Profuse swarms of locusts harass our people and eat out their substance. Each insect himself takes care of his home, grateful to nature that he has a dwelling, and in turn must do his work with labor and joy, helping all fellowkind to achieve a contentment of his labor.

HE HAS KEPT AMONG US, IN TIMES OF PEACE, STANDING ARMIES WITHOUT THE CONSENT OF OUR LEGISLATURE.

HE HAS AFFECTED TO RENDER THE MILITARY INDEPENDENT OF AND SUPERIOR TO THE CIVIL POWER.

Peace is stale within our legislature. Apples are being taken by military independents to be eaten, to be
wasted. Civil power barks across the fence.

Some time ago my dog was beaten on the head . . .
It was said that he growled too loud. . . .
I propose that I be given a muzzle for him and
A bone to cool his brain . . .

FOR QUARTERING LARGE BODIES OF ARMED TROOPS
AMONG US;

The police have invaded the orchards when there is
room in my house for conversation. I proclaim trust.

FOR CUTTING OFF OUR TRADE WITH ALL PARTS OF
THE WORLD;

Many of us have been denied trial by jury for growing our grass out of season. Our tobacco trade has been
cut off in many parts of the world. There is no privacy in our personal lives and, it should be established,
certain boundaries introduce privacy. Our charters and
most valuable laws have been abolished.

HE IS AT THIS TIME TRANSPORTING LARGE ARMIES OF
FOREIGN MERCENARIES TO COMPLETE THE WORKS OF
DEATH, DESOLATION AND TYRANNY, ALREADY BEGUN
WITH CIRCUMSTANCES OF CRUELTY AND PERFIDY
SCARCELY PARALLELED IN THE MOST BARBAROUS AGES,
AND TOTALLY UNWORTHY THE HEAD OF A CIVILIZED NA-
TION.

Our union lacks sophistication. There is no table
grace. Our kitchens are rancid. Death bombs are falling
while we eat our apple pie and cheese. We would like
a new menu.

WE, THE PEOPLE OF THE UNITED STATES, IN ORDER
TO FORM A MORE PERFECT PIE CRUST, ESTABLISH JUS-

TICE, INSURE DOMESTIC TRANQUILITY, PROVIDE FOR ALL
THE GENERAL WELFARE, AND SECURE THE BLESSINGS
WHICH ENHANCE OUR POSTERIOR AND ENABLE US OUR
MOST GLORIOUS CONSTIPATION, THEREFORE RESOLVE
THAT:

there must be a new diet of allegiance,
a hunger that will bring us to terms as gentlemen
and women,
a wish to retire to the country,
of a maid to bring us news of oysters and fish,
of the servants we become to our influence divine
with our particular misfortunes so little,
off to the country to bake our bread,
to get ourselves straight,
to no longer neglect the manners we were given.

I want an end, a conclusion to any further constipation.
I want ideals to have a new sense of gracefulness,
something delivered from the caress of the apples
with a casting out of rotten entrées.
There is time to observe manners of the young and
old,
for our manners have accomplished little for our
lives.
Advanced in sophistication, we conduct the dinner
sitting
with less and less articulation . . . the policy of our
lives is as
badly handled as our country.
We should become primitive in this land of frozen
chicken.
There is richness in becoming aware of others and
with
the sharing of the new opulence around our bread
also is heard a conversation with a new heart.

Does the country bring a renaissance of the family
   we have lost?
It is so simple, so simple that all of the table grace
that has left our fingers could be easily found again.
I must go to all places that are green,
it could be the first time for a peace of mind.
I will keep sending you flowers and strawberries until
   all of you join me . . .

Marc Landy

Born and raised in New York City, twenty-four-year-old Marc Landy attended Oberlin College where "I was editor of *The Activist* and did what I could to give the president of that institution nightmares." A regular contributor to *Commonweal* magazine, he spent a year teaching in New York City public schools and is currently teaching social science at Alice Lloyd College in Pippa Passes, Kentucky.

✛✛✛✛✛✛✛✛✛✛✛✛✛✛✛✛✛✛✛✛✛✛✛✛✛✛✛✛✛✛✛✛✛✛

Our cities are too big and too crowded. We have failed to integrate nonwhite minority groups into our society. Individuals lack a meaningful voice in the decisions that affect their lives, and institutions have become wedded to a set of processes that produce economy of effort and standardization of result rather than concern for individual needs and personal distinction.

It is paradoxical that although many men are agreed that these and other social, economic and political trends are moving this nation to the brink of disaster, they maintain that this situation is due not to the lack of vision on the part of our planners and the lack of courage on the part of our decision makers, but to a series of "problems" that have arisen, *sui generis*, to block our path to the promised land. There is the "urban problem," the "housing problem," the "pollution problem," the "traffic problem" and myriad others. If a "problem" should become particularly thorny, it is then referred to as a "crisis" (for example, in the wake of the 1968 New York teachers' strike, the "urban education problem" became the "urban education crisis"). This phony pragmatic orientation permeates liberal-left thinking, both black and white.

The archetypical urban liberal, John V. Lindsay, ignoring the fact that New York City was being rendered unlivable as a result of racial oppression, overcrowding and poor transit planning, chose to construct a "problem"—administrative reorganization—and devoted the bulk of his tenure in office to "solving" the problem through the creation of superagencies whose functions, it is perhaps superfluous to mention, bear a striking resemblance to their moribund predecessors. Black college students, finding the university irrelevant and impenetrable, have "solved" their problem in the best tradition of American academia. They have sought to create their own Black Studies departments to serve as their very own baronial manors within the feudal system of patronage and property that characterizes the contemporary university.

The same willingness to treat cancer with aspirin that characterizes the "problem" approach to social action has now infected seemingly more radical modes of analysis and action. The Yippies and the radical lifestylers seem to believe that a mere demonstration of how to live the free, nonhypocritical life will be sufficient to change public attitudes. (Billy Graham has a similar faith in "blowing minds".) The Black Panthers and other community groups seem to act on the premise that this country's most powerful decision makers wear a policeman's uniform. Both the mind blowers and the pig hunters seem to accept the premise that in this post-Freudian, media-dominated age the easiest and perhaps the only way to achieve social change is through personality manipulation. This triumph of mind over matter leads to the acceptance of appearance for reality.

The increased standardization of tasks in our economy has been successfully veiled by the men's fashion revolution, which has given employees the opportunity to clothe their lack of vocational distinction in the increased distinctiveness of their attire. A moustache and an Edwardian suit do not really make life as a key punch operator any more satisfying.

The doting mother-child relationship that exists between the media and student protestors ("Just phone us when you plan to occupy a building or throw a stink bomb and we'll have a camera crew right there") has allowed the demonstrators themselves, not to mention the public at large, to mistake militant tactics for radical vision (we *must* have done something important, we got a spot on all the major networks). An other worldly asceticism, rivaled only by the Christian martyrs and Buddhist monks, has been evolved by those "radicals" who profess a contempt for the limited goals of militant liberals. They plan to wait until the whole "Military-Industrial Complex, Corporate-Bureaucratic System" has been brought to its knees in an Armageddon of broken brass and spindled IBM cards to start to build the kingdom of God on earth.

A direct attack upon the content and character of irresponsible, uncontrolled and impersonal decision making has been launched by diverse groups who share a mistrust of large institutions and a concern for the concrete rather than the psychic. The McCarthy Presidential campaign sought to go beyond articulation of opposition against the war in Vietnam to a critique of the overcentralization of power in the hands of the President and a search for new means of involving the citizen in political activity. The militant members of the National Farmers Organization have sought to decentralize the oligopolistic food industry by replacing impersonal market criteria with bargaining power for small entrepreneurs. The word *technology* is no longer a synonym for righteousness. Students and faculty at MIT and other R&D-dominated campuses are demanding that research allocations be determined with regard to social priorities and that these priorities be arrived at democratically.

The community control movement, the most powerful of the groups advocating limitation of centralized, bureaucratic authority, has arisen where the failure of that form of control has been the most pronounced—in our major cities. The demand for community control of goods and services rests on the most basic, but also the most radical and ambiguous, tenet of democratic theory: those most directly affected by institutions should control them. It has now become fashionable in left-wing circles to demand community control of everything from health care to the police force. It is less fashionable to ask what constitutes a community, and what sorts of processes are amenable to any sort of public control. How exactly does a community control a heart surgeon or a tactical patrol force?

The inability to deal with these two questions has led to the failure of attempts at community control to date. It is impossible to democratize an assembly line; it is equally impossible to democratize an educational processing plant. Although "control" of the Ocean Hill–Brownsville school district was given over (at least temporarily) to elements of the community, little thought was directed to restructuring the system itself to make control possible. Class sizes were not reduced and thus teachers remained strangers to their children. The hallways of old school buildings continued to resemble cell blocks while classes were in session, and the Long Island Expressway at rush hour during recesses. While the central board and the local board wrangled over who was formally in charge, the logic of the factory continued to rule the classroom. The Ocean Hill experiment died before the state legislature killed it, because the governing board had sought merely to control the personnel who ran the schools rather than to create community schools.

Proponents of community control assume that it will operate within the urban context as presently defined. They fail to realize that the same factors that have made contemporary urban life unbearable will serve also to strangle these "community within the city" experiments.

The standard contemporary model of a city is as a "network of communications." This model supplants older ones which looked upon the city as a "center for trade," and then as a "hub of manufacture." Just as changes in trade and production techniques rendered the previous models obsolete, so modern systems of telecommunications make the present model an anachronism. It is no longer true that people need to reside and work near each other in order to keep in touch. In order to escape from this "planned obsolescence" type of model, urbanists like Jane Jacobs have conjured up an image of the city as a "center for contact." They see the genius of the city residing in its ability to allow different types of people to rub up against each other in a variety of contexts. The lie is given to this model by the almost frantic attempt of most urban dwellers to avoid any form of contact they consider unfamiliar or threatening, either by withdrawing into ethnic enclaves or by fleeing to the suburbs.

To find a more adequate conception of the city it might be rewarding to look back to the most successful cities in history, those of the Greeks. The Greek word for city was *polis*, which may be translated as "polity." The purpose of the Greek city was to provide for the common good. The terms "city" and "community" were synonymous. The city was a political rather than a geographic or an economic entity; it had citizens, not residents. Clearly no contemporary American city fits this model. In an age of rapid mobility, one's address is considered a temporary accident rather than a political decision. However, if we are to wrest control over our environment from the "iron hand" of technocratic logic and restore it to the "community," we must somehow infuse our notion of contiguous residence with a sense of common loyalty and purpose.

The first step in this endeavor is to distinguish a community from a neighborhood. A neighborhood is what people go home to in the evening. By definition, it lacks the resources to provide for the common good and security of its residents. The major test of a community is whether or not it contains a variety of institutions that are really worth controlling. The willingness of foundations and corporations to underwrite local control of small businesses and elementary schools stems from their conviction that the impact of these institutions does not exceed beyond the neighborhood. Such gifts are considered safe and trivial. A true community would be able to tax these dubious benefactors rather than be forced to rely on their largesse.

The geographical partitioning of our cities into functional units makes community control impossible. We have neighborhoods that lack the necessary diversity to exist as anything but parasites, and commercial and manufacturing districts that are so crowded and polluted, and whose land values are so overinflated, that any physical restructuring of these areas is out of the question. If our present cities do not provide adequate ground for communities to take root, let us institute carefully coordinated programs of population resettlement and decentralization.

Of all forms of planning, resettlement is greeted with the most public and scholarly resistance. To induce people to move (unless it is to kick poor people out of tenements in order to "urban renew") is considered to be an invasion of personal freedom. To maintain that people freely chose to live in the city is to assume that they had other options. In fact, they were compelled to migrate to the city because that was the only place where vocational and commercial opportunities and a decent level of social services were to be found. In the past, resettlement has been attempted only among rural peoples who have had great attachment to the land and whose ancestors lived in the vicinity. On the other hand, a large proportion of city dwellers grew up in rural settings, and most urbanites neither own land in the city nor can trace their urban heritage further back than one generation. The city, and the neighborhoods that compose it, is still an alien phenomenon to most of its inhabitants. Their heritage is still largely a rural one. Planned resettlement would, at worst, represent a different form of compulsion from the kind that drove people to the city.

The resettlement of people into small, functionally integrated communities is now technologically feasible. Recent advances permit the escape from crowded, centralized forms of living. Modern forms of telecommunications, transport and techniques of energy utilization, manufacturing and marketing make it possible for most forms of goods and services to be provided by small, decentralized facilities. Currently, 60 percent of America's population occupies only 7½ percent of its land. If half that number could be dispersed among the underpopulated 92½ percent of the land in small, community-controlled new towns, the revitalization of our present cities could be easily accomplished.

As previously mentioned, public policy is currently designed to ameliorate "problems" and "crises," not to implement a common vision of the good life. As a consequence, we are stuck with massive programs that most people oppose in principle. Our most extensive program of aid to the poor—welfare—is considered degrading and dehumanizing by both the public and the recipients themselves. Our public housing program consists of large, high-rise buildings, the very sort of residence that our more affluent citizens have "voted against" by moving to the suburbs. These programs are allowed to continue because they are easy to implement and cause minimum disturbance to the bulk of the population who are not directly affected by them. If we *believe* that public institutions should be democratically controlled, then they must be limited in size and complexity to a degree that permits public scrutiny, even at the cost of decreased service and efficiency. If we are convinced that certain engines of technology, the gun and the automobile, for example, threaten public safety, poison the air and make our cities unlivable, then we must restrict their use and ownership even if this violates cherished notions of personal freedom.

Our current crop of "problems" and "crises" are a direct consequence of the role that we have assigned to public policy in general. Before we consider various schemes for restructuring, rehumanizing and decentralizing our institutions, we must first decide that public policy should, in fact, be the embodiment of our most common values, even if it limits private autonomy and convenience.

Les Leopold

Born in Vineland, New Jersey, in 1947, Mr. Leopold worked for Eugene McCarthy during the 1968 Presidential campaign as a member of the national staff and as head of the crowd staff for Southern California. He is presently an intern in the New Jersey Urban Education Corps working toward an M.A. in urban teaching.

✚✚✚

I

This is a warning to the Nixon Administration: Do not repress the activism that is causing the unrest on college campuses today. This activism, which is usually represented by SDS, is but a small fraction of a deep-rooted unrest. A much larger group of students are at the moment disorganized, submerged and generally apathetic. However, any catalyst, such as a wave of repression, might galvanize these students into a potent and volatile political force. This larger group is on the fringe of the political system. They are at the moment unwilling to participate in the tactics that SDS employs. And they are uncertain that the political system, with its electoral politics, can provide the meaningful social change they feel our society desperately needs.

In most cases these are the same students who rallied to the support of Senator Eugene McCarthy. These are students from middle-class liberal homes, who had always considered themselves liberals, but who have taken a turn to the left. This departure from their liberal backgrounds, I feel, is in large part a result of their activities in the last Presidential campaign. After the Democratic convention, these students felt thoroughly alienated from the two-party system. How did they get that way? What did they experience and per-ceive during the campaign that contributed to their present condition? I am one of these students, and I would like to describe the political education we received through our own efforts, and how it has contributed to the opinions we now hold.

Most of us joined the McCarthy movement out of a desire to bring the war in Vietnam to an end. Most of us left the movement with a deep-seated commitment to change the fundamental structure of the American political and economic system.

II

To a Northerner, Atlanta is a surprising city. Its skyscrapers and bleach-white Peachtree Center, its rolling hills and visible wealth are reminiscent of Westchester County, New York. However, at close inspection one uncovers nine or ten dilapidated service ghettos (including two white ones), which are totally unconnected to each other through public transportation. Yet from five to seven each morning, one can watch thousands of women wait in line for the buses that quickly shuttle them out to the suburbs for household work.

We Northerners had just finished the primary route with a victory in New York. Our spirits were high, and we were sent down to the South to solicit support for McCarthy from the black community, to help improve his lily-white image; and, of course, we felt that the blacks belonged in our wing of the Democratic Party.

Through some quick espionage work we gathered a list of potential black supporters and arranged interviews with them. Our first greeting was a resounding slap in the face. A twenty-six-year-old junior-executive trainee and executive member of the Atlanta Metro Summit Leadership Conference (a conglomeration of all the civil rights groups in Atlanta) sat down and began lecturing us on the evils of Northern white liberals, and how we had no business soliciting black support for anything. He asked us why we were sent down there and why the organization had not hired any black organizers. We told him we were volunteers. He then pointed out to us an alarming and quite obvious fact: that the McCarthy campaign could not expect black support because black people had to work full time in the summer, especially if they were students, and that black housewives were often the breadwinners in the families and had no time for volunteer work. In short, the volunteer campaign meant, by definition, an all-white campaign. The meeting came to an embarrassing close. (Our lunch had not arrived in time, since the restaurant had no intention of rapidly serving an integrated table.)

After a few more interviews it became apparent that without money we were totally lost. Poor people in our party system were not about to get involved in an ill-funded insurgency movement.

We did receive some money; it was tied, however, to the planning of an airport rally for McCarthy to be held on July 18. Rallies are a major concern of most political campaigns. Ours was no different, so for that we had money. Rallies were my specialty; I had been in charge of building crowds in Southern California during the primary. We had a system whereby we would contact organized groups and offer them transportation to the airport to see McCarthy. Throughout the campaign we had had a hard time attracting black people. In Atlanta we were in big trouble; the airport was ten miles away, and, of course, there was no public transportation from the inner city. However, we were fortunate, because of another deplorable economic fact of the city: most black teen-agers and summer-school students had never seen the airport. We contacted the principals and teachers who were conducting special summer education sessions in the inner city, and the response was overwhelming. Teachers were more than eager to show their classes their famous airport, and McCarthy too. And we were eager, since the voting age in Georgia is eighteen. The result was a success. McCarthy received the largest airport rally in the history of Atlanta, and the audience was 50 percent black.

We thought we were moving in the right direction. However, some of the older members of the organization back in Washington thought we had gone too far. What might not have been apparent to the general public was the fantastic split that was growing within the McCarthy movement between the young and the old. After the primaries some of the old-line Democrats became very unhappy with our participation in the organization. We were pushing the war issue too far, we were too eager to offend the regular Southern Democrats with our positions on the race issues. But we had just gotten into politics, and we were not about to be thrown out by our own organization. Thanks to some crafty politics by the Senator's daughter Mary, we were allowed to continue. However, the fight was just beginning for us in Atlanta.

We wanted to help to overthrow the regular Democratic Party of Georgia (Lester Maddox included) and to present a challenge delegation to the convention. We had the perfect opportunity coming up in mid-July when the Georgia Democratic Forum, a left-of-the-party group, was going to hold its convention. However, we just could not get the go-ahead. Instead of spreading throughout the state and gathering support for a challenge slate, we were asked by Washington to do research on the Maddox delegation. It seems incredible, but for the first five weeks of my stay in Georgia it seemed as if we were going to count on successfully wooing the Maddox delegation. Yet we were covering our bets by wooing Julian Bond simultaneously. I was greatly disheartened and disillusioned, to say the least. Finally, one week before the convention we got the go-ahead to challenge, and challenge we did. It appeared that our lobbying had worked again.

The creation of the Georgia challenge delegation was a delight to those who believed that a new party based on grass roots democracy was possible. For the first time since the Reconstruction poor black people and poor white people were participating in the selection of delegates to a national convention. A thousand people attended, and a slate was elected by a district that was half black and mostly poor. This may have been the most positive political experience in the campaign, for it clearly taught us that party politics, especially reform and radical party politics, had a definite future in the South.

What about the North? Next stop: Chicago.

III

By the time I reached Chicago I was exhausted, and somewhat disillusioned with our candidate. I was extremely upset with his decision to ask young people to stay away from Chicago so that there would not be any trouble. I felt this was a betrayal of the antiwar movement because it isolated those who came to Chicago as non-McCarthyites and militants, which was simply not the case. Nevertheless, I was determined to see McCarthy through Chicago, to stick it out to the end. In retrospect, I think a good deal of the violence could have been avoided by having thousands of these students in Chicago because they would have moderated the movement leadership, and they almost certainly would have received a parade permit since they would have had McCarthy's backing.

I am not going to describe the violence or the convention, because they have been described quite adequately by many others. Rather I would like to tell about what the McCarthy students were thinking, and how they were affected by what they personally perceived.

First of all, a good many of us were having ideological conflicts within ourselves. Since we were most definitely allied with the antiwar demonstrators outside the Hilton Hotel, we were wondering why we should not go outside and join them. Our candidate was surely a loser; wouldn't we be contributing most by going outside? Should we work in the system or outside the system? Most of us never did answer the question. But for many it was really the first time they had asked it. When the violence came, the question became more acute, and more of us began to lean to the left. And when the convention was over, there were almost no regular Democrats left on the staff (and, to be sure, no Republicans).

Second, most of us could not believe the blatant manipulation we saw. We were new to party politics. The deals were appalling to us, just as they were to the good-government reformers of the early twentieth century. Daley's party simply was not ours. But more importantly, we could not believe the attitude of the delegates. We were in close contact with them and saw how little they actually perceived about us. They were scared. The army and the police were outside, and these young kids were inside causing trouble. We were communists or pinkos in their eyes, and we deserved what we got.

And finally, we were profoundly affected by the violence. It was truly incredible. Was this the system we supported, where political rallies were snuffed out like the labor strikes of our earlier history? But wasn't this the same party that was conducting the war in Vietnam, and weren't these troops of the same army? And weren't these delegates the same men who received the bonuses and overtime from the defense contracts? The picture began to come in clear. We might not have the opportunity to answer the question, in the system or out of it. We might just be kicked out of it if we spoke too loudly or organized too strongly. We would remember the blood for a long time.

We went in as middle-class liberals. We left as middle-class leftists. The party was rotten. The war was rotten. We saw in Atlanta and in the country's other large ghettos the agonies of our welfare state. We saw in our own organization and in Chicago how far away the goal of party reform really was. And we saw in the streets the price we might have to pay in the future if we went too far.

IV

And now let me return to my warning to the Nixon Administration: You are not the Democratic Party, and we expect even less of your Administration. The cities will get worse during the next four years. Economic justice will not be a product of your Administration. But we fear a wave of repression will be. And if repression hits the campuses, it will do just the opposite of what you desire. You may eliminate SDS, but you will organize us, and the campuses will look like little Chicagos.

As I write this today, two college administrations in northern Ohio (Oberlin and Kent State) are trying to eliminate radical dissent. Although they have succeeded in suspending the obvious troublemakers, they have aroused the silent students around the issue of due process. The tactics of SDS are now starting to spread to the more moderate groups. The administrations feared disruption, and now they have created more.

Ricnard Lorber

Richard Lober and his uncle wrote *The Gap*, a best-selling generational dialogue that received some attention in *Life*, etc., and was even sold to the movies. A twenty-three-year-old graduate of Columbia College, he is presently living and writing in New York's Upper West Side, "body-thinking as much as head-thinking . . . getting into the *Tactilectual* . . . hearing the death rattle of the rational tradition all around me in the air. . . ."

✛✛

Richard a b c d e f g h ı j k l M. Nixon wears boxer shorts with little color pictures of tanks and violins. In this afternoon heat, words melt in our mouths and tanks and violins stick to his sweaty thighs. Pat has the good common sense to wear Carter's cotton underpanties. Very absorbent.

Waiting, watching, whispering, we were all around Richard Milhous Nixon going to the dentist. Many questions dented the soft licorice tar, questions steaming up from the steamy asphalt street, questions of what was "just routine," questions that could not be answered by white-walled toothless limousines, helicopters, motor scooters, roller skaters.

Dr. W. Campbell Hudson, Sr.?

W. Campbell Hudson, Jr.?

What is the a b c d e f g h i j k l m n o p q r s t u v W?

Dear Mr. Richard (M.) Nixon:

It has been called to our attention that your "milhous" lacks an "e" or needs no "s." People are talking. People are saying: "Could it be that 'Milhous' is truly the plural of 'Milhou,' which is to say, 'Milhou's'? And could it be that with an 'e' he'd have a residence instead of a name?" Let us not confuse the "Milhouse" with the Whitehouse, but, Mr. R. M's. N., upon retirement will you return to the singular? Will you strike the "s" or add the "e"? If you add the "e" and make a "Milhouse," upon termination of your lease as commander-in-chief, will you sublet the "Milhouse" and move the Whitehouse into your name? Or "Whitehous"? Until further notification from your man all inquiries will be channeled into our file "M," arranged alphabetically in the folder "Miscellaneous" at the end of file "M." Upon receipt of seven or more inquiries, typed, double-spaced, we will prepare a special folder under the heading "Milhou's." Mr. President, we wait to be advised.

Respectfully,

(seven hundred Magic Marker signatures)

P.S. It has been called to our attention that you have ever so craftily steered a middle course between "Milhouse" and "Milhou" with "Milhou's" (read "Milhous"). We are in awe!

Aunt Carlata was with us in the crowd. She noted your eloquently expressive hands. Of course, she had only seen pictures. Which reminded me of pictures too. Your open palms, your open mouth, your fingers stretching out like the little onion sprouts that grow in the vegetable compartment of our Frigidaire. And when you smile your thumbs grow rigid, their tips bend back, little noses on each hand. The wide spaces between your sprouting fingers, your scallion digits, and the gray-greenish puss hue of your unclipped translucent fingernail tips suggest to Aunt Carlata that you are a very open person. I don't see it. Then again, I couldn't see your fingernail tips. There was, not unhappily, some disagreement among us. James, who can read palms, said you have a lifeline. Monseigneur Jørgne, who taught James how to read palms, said your lifeline is badly effaced by that paste you smear all over your palms. Ricky-the-Kid confirmed this and added, to the chagrin of some former friends, that you don't have any fingerprints either.

As for myself, I used to wear briefs, with a roomy pouch and an elastic band that had red and blue threads of rubber woven into the otherwise white cotton elastic band. But after you lost to a b c d e f g h i j k, J. F. K., I switched in sympathy to boxer shorts. Grandma has scoured Bathgate Avenue but she just can't seem to come up with tanks and violins. I've got horseshoes and dachshunds and daffodils, airplanes and bathtubs, polka dots and capybaras, casaba melons and garlic cloves and escarole and acorn squash and sour green tomatoes, artists' renderings of biblical characters and pastel princess phones, and even one pair with little cowboy bullets and midget Mexican men serenading older women on inexpensive factory-made mandolins, all in different earth colors. That's pretty close— it's as close as Grandma has come—but it's still not tanks and violins. Although on sweaty days like this, even aircraft and vegetable nutrients and dark-complexioned Midwesterners and snapshots of God stick to one's thighs.

Consensus of opinion in the crowd was that the Carter's cotton underpanties worn by Pat Nixon this afternoon have been strategic in your career. People were saying you married Pat Nixon for her name, for the prinking poignancies of nostalgia ever recalling you to those odoriferous days when you sang:

> I see London,
> I see France,
> I see Patti's underpants.
> Are they blue?
> Are they pink?
> I can't tell,
> But boy, oh, boy, they do stink!

In fact, Carter's come in white, pink, daffodil and pistachio green. Regatta blue has been discontinued. And I personally have little or no use for Carter's cotton underpants even if they are very absorbent on a wilting, melting, damp, limp afternoon.

We waited.

From time to time your men came by with words of ease for our anxieties, with reports to raise our spirits, with refreshments and relief and a piquant scent, with sentences spoken from the mouth, the heart: "Just routine, JUST ROUTINE, JUST ROUTINE!"

Your helicopter. Carlata and James and Jørgne saw it on a color television that was making pictures in only black and white. So while we were waiting we guessed its colors. Although I hadn't seen it in color, I knew it was black. All shiny black, like an onyx mirror with a spray-stippled grain that gave all reflections a nice fleshy texture so that you could shave in the sheen of its fuselage and the reflection of your face in the fuselage looked more like your face than your face in flesh. Being stranded in a South American rain forest with a helicopter like that is no hardship at all. I asked your man where I might get some of that black. He advised against it, said it was less than expedient, insufficiently efficient, he wouldn't tell me where. Hadn't I noticed the lemon and lime shaving cream behind "the Mr. President's" left ear lobe? Your man was convinced that bathroom mirrors can't be beat. It was true. I have never had toothpaste stains on my tie or on my gloves.

Sometimes I felt very alone in the crowd. Like when the other 699 started cheering and chanting a tune of "Just routine." "Can't we exchange hi's again some-time," I thought aloud. Then the band, the Marine Band, got into the swing. They love playing for Richard Milhou's Nixon. He has so many names: Dick, Richard, Rich, Richie, Dickie, Ricky, Rick, Ricardo, Ri, Dicko, Dicky, Dicker, et cetera. Like playing for a whole regiment of commanders-in-chief. The many "Mil-hou's." And such a good marcher, even on sand, when the Marines go to the seashore to play for him under the browning, baking, Florida Key, Caribbean sun. Swinging his arms in rhythm with the swing of the band of Marines, syncopated palms, to-fro, to-fro, to-fro. And marching gives our President terrific arches. Adding inches to his height, raising his head above the crowd. No one will ever again accuse R. M.'s. N. of being a flatfoot. Certainly not with his band around. Dr. Scholl, you can retire, we won't be needing you for a while.

W. Campbell Hudson, D.D.S., yes, then, now and again.

Then was when R. M.'s. N. lost to a b c d e f g h i J. F. K. and everybody was laughing and singing, Nix on Nixon, Nix on Nixon. People were saying he went to the dentist to fix his smile. It didn't help. After a b c d e f g h i j k l m n o p q R. M.'s. N. lost to a b c d e f g h i j k, J. F. K., even I was saying: "If only you were Nixin or Noxon we could spell you backward, and upside down, yes, but for a slight ir-regularity in the capital "N" we could spell you back-ward and even upside down; using a small "n" would be better yet, would read better backward and upside down, less irregularity, it would be more suitable and preferable potentially in any case."

Crowds would chant:

"Nix on Nixon, Nox on Nixin, Nix on Noxin, Nix on Nixin, Nox on Noxon, Nox in Noxon, Nix in Nixin, Nix in Noxin, Nox in Nixin, Nox in Nixon, Noxon, Nixin, Noxin, Nixon, Nix on Nixon, Noxon, Nixin, Noxon, Nixin, Noxon, Nixon, Noxin. Milhouse Noxin."

And W. Campbell Hudson, Sr., D.D.S. took his pointy little tool in hand and picked the letters from your teeth, that were caught in your teeth, and told you to stay away from farmer "chees" and carraway seeds, and now here you are with a shiny black helicopter with a colorful seal on its right-side door near where you shave, where you brush your teeth.

A seal not unlike the tourist sticker we got when we visited Fort McHenry and the Thousand Islands and the St. Lawrence Seaway. I soaked the circular Fort McHenry seal in rusty water in a cereal bowl. The see-through seal slithered off like wet cellophane, which it was, leaving only a slimy rectangle of shiny wet paper, which was limp and which I disregarded. Then I scooped up the seal into my palm and made a mad dash for the rear window of Dad's '54 Chevy, before Fort McHenry dried. It looked really good there on the back window, and wouldn't you know it, sure enough, an officer of the police informed Dad that it was a violation since it obstructed rear vision and unless it were removed he would find it necessary to give Dad a summons the next time he saw us with the seal, even if it was Fort McHenry.

Mr. President, I hope you didn't put that seal on your helicopter all by yourself! I mean, I mean, I just naturally expected that your man would do it. I mean

I know it means a lot to you, but you're the President and . . .

The rumor shot through the crowd, from ear to ear, like shock waves of lightning on a putrid garden, like a pulsing strobe light on decay-soft vegetables, flashing white and rotting in a warm polluted rain . . .

"Nixon doesn't brush after every meal!" He's just been using Listerine, even after garlic breakfasts.

Your shiny black helicopter must now bring you to the dentist. Speeding you from your private office, where, on a decorator color telephone you speak to astronauts, to your Armstrong, your Man-on-the-Moon. In the black and white pictures on our color television it seemed that your phone was a natural neutral, a shade of beige. Could I be wrong? Was it actually daisy yellow, or chalk or bone ochre or persimmon? While watching the live astronaut movie in our home on our teevee, words and letters flashed across the bottom of the screen:

Astronauts Hoisting Rock Boxes . . . A. H. R. B.

All P.L.S.S.'s (Portable Life Support Systems; *editor's note*) were go. I dreamed of the day when they will be in pastel decorator colors to match telephones. But I dream now all the time. And before I knew it the commencement of E.V.A. (Extra Vehicular Activities; *editor's note*) termination had been terminated, and the termination, commenced and terminated. And the movie was over without a C.L.S. (Crew Loss Situation; *editor's note*), which meant the rocket ship didn't crash and the spacemen didn't all get killed. And you were speeding, Mr. Richard Milhou's Nixon, despite the warning of the N.I.M.H. (National Institute of Mental Health; *editor's note*) that speed kills, you were speeding to the dentist, W. Campbell Hudson, Sr., D.D.S., to have the letters that get stuck in your teeth picked out with a sharp, pointy tool!

With all this speeding there is no time for brushing, for dry underwear. Nevetheless, space exploration would seem to be a viable pursuit.

Many in the crowd similarly have no time for these characteristic and calciferous upper and lower case revelations. Unaware of their consequences they simply ask: "Is there no Water Pik in the Whitehouse?" Waiting was becoming religious in the heat. And your man tells us it is "just routine."

Billy Graham preaches every morning after an allstar breakfast of raisins and Wheaties ("Breakfast of Champions") and "B" compound vitamin pill. Then he brushes.

For my own part, I find that gargling Chlorox is a real eye-opener before my Kelloggs Special "K" and after Special "K," and others among us, some 17 to 26 out of the other 699 in the crowd, do from time to time gargle Chlorox, as well as, and heed this Mr. R. M.'s N., as well as brushing at least three to seven times a day!

Pycopay Brushes have the C.D.T. (Council on Dental Therapeutics; *editor's note*) of the A.D.A.-recommended number of bristles, two rows of six bristle bundles each, and in both the natural bristle and nylon varieties there are different custom-manufactured bristle strengths: *soft, medium, hard, extra hard,* except in nylon where there is also an *extra soft,* which is as supple as *soft* in natural, and proceeding from this Natural–Nylon Suppleness Differential (N.N.S.D.) for natural bristle ratings commensurate to the nylon, read *medium* for *soft,* read *hard* for *medium,* read *extra hard* for *hard* and read *cut-up gums, stripped enamel* in natural for *extra hard* in nylon. Not that I would suggest this last reading in natural or nylon for Mr. R. M.'s. Nixon, but we all agree these bristles clean down to the whitest white and this can be politically expeditious. One must, however, be attentive to the consequences of bristle overrigidity: abraded tongue (taste buds go numb), receding gums. Pasty, punctured cheek blisters and palate burns are outside of the N.N.S.D. frame of reference, albeit, inside the mouth.

Seven hundred of us discussed these and other toothsome problems which you as President must swallow each morning and taste throughout the day, with your Swiss Style Ovaltine and unsweetened Cheerios, your alphabet soup Madrilène, your coddled minute steak and café-cinnamon-au-lait, your Sanka and Oleomargarine and Wonder Bread, your White Rose tea and cold shrimp scampi, your Medaglio D'Oro espresso and Peter Pan Peanut Butter Chunk Style and citrated caffeine tablet, your breakfast lamb, with mint jam.

These problems you taste are National Contingencies, within the orbit of domestic and international welfare and well-being. These problems may be as your man has said, "just routine." But they are, Mr. President R. M.'s. N., as Rapunzel has said, "your problems!"

And as Professor Nietzchze, the possessor of a great Teutonic Philologic Romantic Philosophic mind, has said, has, that is, pointed out in a digression on the Shakespearian scholarship of Heinrich Albatross, your Man-on-the-Moon, your "Armstrong," is, polylingually speaking, none other than our own latter-day Fortinbras! With the triumph of Prince Armstrong, with the hoisting of rock boxes on the moon, with the advent of your beige (?) Geo-Lunar intracommuniqué, tanks and violins are no longer, can no longer be construed as, have no longer the ho-hum linearity and colorless irrelevance of that which is "just routine"! Those of us who watched for your seal, who swooned in the helicoidal gale of your synthetic black waterproof whirlybird, are astringently aware of the triumph of Fortinbras. Yes, Hamlet is dead. Yet, Mr. R. M.'s. N., *the rest* we have agreed must not be *Silencio*! Despite the as yet unknown identity of Dr. W. Campbell Hudson, Sr.'s Christian name, the identity of W. Campbell Hudson, Jr., his son, WE WILL NOT BE TRADUCED!

It must be said firmly and finally, with a tongueload of candor, with a cavity of rancor, Mr. President, WE REJECT GARLIC AND LISTERINE. And dentifrice will not do.

Mr. President, Mr. P. R. M's. N., . . ., you have bad breath.

Rod Manis

Rod Manis is twenty-seven years old and presently a research associate at the Hoover Institution on War, Revolution and Peace at Stanford University. Manis has been an area director for the Los Angeles County Republican Central Committee, chairman of California Young Americans for Freedom, chairman of Sacramento County Youth for Goldwater, alternate delegate to the 1963 Young Republican National Convention, and in the summer of 1966 he visited India for the World Youth Crusade for Freedom (Freedom Corps) to work with anticommunist youth groups. As chairman of the UCLA Council for a Volunteer Military, he appeared on several radio and TV shows (Joe Pyne et al.) to urge abolition of the draft. "I am happy only with the title 'libertarian,' but free market economist is also acceptable. I am certainly not a conservative, right-winger, etc. . . ."

✠✠✠✠✠✠✠✠✠✠✠✠✠✠✠✠✠✠✠✠✠✠✠✠✠✠✠✠✠✠✠✠✠✠

"The scarlet thread running through the thoughts and actions of people all over the world is the delegation of great problems to all-absorbing leviathan—the state. . . . Every time that we try to lift a problem to the government, to the same extent we are sacrificing the liberties of the people."
—John F. Kennedy
(Boston *Post*, April 23, 1950)

Today we are facing an intellectual crisis.[1] The easy, pat answers of the 1930s and the decades of "liberal" control have not solved the problems of poverty at

---

[1] See Professor Stephen Tonsor's speech, "On Living at the End of an Era," to the 1968 Annual Meeting of the Philadelphia Society, Chicago. (Copies are available from Young Americans for Freedom, 1221 Massachusetts Avenue, Washington, D.C. 20005.)

home or brought peace abroad.[2] My generation is intensely aware of this failure.

Two important forces are at work. First, intellectuals, especially the young, are becoming increasingly aware of the fact that big, powerful and expensive government is not the automatic answer to all of our problems. At best, such government is incompetent to come to grips with the problems facing us; at worst, it is a tool of special interests and compounds and multiplies our difficulties.

Second, our parents went through a severe depression and world war. They emerged with a strong desire for security: a steady job, marriage, a home in the suburbs and conformity. Their children grew up in these safe, secure homes and today want freedom instead. They want the freedom to choose their own ideas, live their own lives, see and enjoy the world, try out the unusual, learn and change, dream and build.

Where we *are* going, though certainly not everyone is yet aware of it, and where we *should* be going is toward more individual freedom. This is the theme running through the thoughts and actions of my generation. Man's great hope is that we will get there.

Freedom exists to the extent that a man can use his property (broadly defined to include his life, body, personal possessions, ideas or anything of value to him) any way he wishes, so long as he does not infringe upon the property rights of others. The only purpose and function of the government is to protect these property rights. Much of human misery can be attributed to the failure of government to protect or the actual infringement by government itself on these rights.

[2] See Daniel P. Moynihan's speech before the Americans for Democratic Action in Washington (reprinted in Los Angeles *Times*, October 1, 1967, Section G, pp. 1-2). Also see the article by Richard Goodwin (speechwriter for JFK and Eugene McCarthy) in *Commentary* (June, 1967).

Libertarians are those who wish to maximize personal and economic freedom; authoritarians wish to minimize it. Classical liberals (Locke, Smith, Jefferson, Mill, Mencken) were libertarians.[3] Classical liberalism achieved its greatest influence in the nineteenth century with these results: (1) free trade and laissez-faire brought the greatest period of economic growth in human history[4]; (2) the nineteenth century saw the longest period of peace in modern history; (3) slavery and serfdom were abolished and colonialism came to a halt.

But authoritarianism and government intervention still existed in some ways and from them came evils that were, unfortunately, blamed upon free enterprise and libertarianism. By the late 1800s it was widely believed that "unrestrained" laissez-faire had led to monopolies and cartels in industry and railroads. But,

[3] See John Locke's *The Second Treatise of Government*, Adam Smith's *The Wealth of Nations*.

Thomas Jefferson, in his First Inaugural Address, said: "Sometimes it is said that man cannot be trusted with the government of himself. Can he, then, be trusted with the government of others? Or have we found angels in the form of kings to govern him? Let history answer this question. If we can prevent the government from wasting the labors of the people, under the pretense of caring for them, they will be happy."

John Stuart Mill: "The only freedom which deserves the name is that of pursuing our own good in our own way, so long as we do not attempt to deprive others of theirs or impede their efforts to obtain it."

See also Murray N. Rothbard, "H. L. Mencken: The Joyous Libertarian," *The New Individualist Review* (Summer, 1962).

[4] See Karl Marx, *The Communist Manifesto* (Chicago, Regnery, 1954), pp. 21-23. "The bourgeoisie, by the rapid improvement of all instruments of production, by the immensely facilitated means of communication, draws all, even the most barbarian, nations into civilization.

"The bourgeoisie, during its rule of scarce one hundred years, has created more massive and more colossal productive forces than have all preceding generations together."

in fact, it was government that devised tariffs and quotas to protect some firms from competition and, at the same time, gave land grants and special privileges to railroads. In California the Southern Pacific Railroad controlled the state legislature. State law protected Southern Pacific's monopoly by prohibiting any other line from building into port cities. The Democratic national platform of 1888 said that tariffs and quotas were the "mother of monopoly," and urged their reduction.

But instead of ending this intervention, it was increased. Antitrust laws and railroad regulations (under the Interstate Commerce Commission) were supposed to protect consumers. The opposite was the result. Antitrust laws have blocked the expansion of efficient firms, retarding progress and holding up prices.[5] The ICC and other regulatory agencies were taken over by the interests they were supposed to regulate and used government power to keep out competition and to raise prices.[6]

[5] See Robert H. Bork, "The Supreme Court Versus Corporate Efficiency," in *Fortune*, vol. LXXVI (August, 1967), pp. 92-94, 155-56, 158. Professor Bork analyzes the Proctor & Gamble Supreme Court decision and its ramifications, which he calls a "manifestation of long-term trends in antitrust. The Supreme Court has steadily and drastically reshaped the law to protect the inefficient producer at the expense of consumers."

In a case decided by Judge Learned Hand, Circuit Court of Appeals (CCA 2d), 1944. (U.S. vs. Alcoa, 148 F. 2nd. 416 (1945), Judge Hand ruled that efficiency is almost a crime. Alcoa insisted that it "never excluded competitors; but we think of no more effective exclusion than progressively to embrace each new opportunity as it opened, and to face every newcomer with new capacity already geared into a great organization, having the advantage of experience, trade connections, and the elite of personnel."

[6] See George W. Hilton, "The Consistancy of the Interstate Commerce Act," in *Journal of Law and Economics*, vol. IX (October, 1966), p. 87. Also, Christopher D. Stone,

A whole generation grew up on the myth that the great depression of the 1930s was the result of unregulated free enterprise. However, Professor Milton Friedman has shown that depressions are caused by a decline in the rate of growth of the money supply. Between 1929 and 1932 the Federal Reserve System caused and allowed the money supply to fall by one fourth, the largest monetary and economic contraction in our history. Although such regulation has been sold to us as a cure for booms and depressions, we have had much more economic instability since the creation of the Federal Reserve than in the previous, relatively freer period. Conflicting and archaic bank regulation has significantly reduced banking competition and efficiency.[7]

The trend away from classical liberalism or libertarianism reached its height in Nazi Germany and Communist Russia and China. Although the growth rates of these countries are often cited as support for

"ICC: Some Reminiscences on the Future of American Transportation"; Sam Peltzman, "CAB: Freedom from Competition"; Robert M. Hurt, "FCC: Free Speech, 'Public Needs,' and Mr. Minow," in *New Individualist Review*, vol. II (Spring, 1963), pp. 3-37 and R. H. Coase, "The Federal Communications Commission," in *Journal of Law and Economics*, vol. II (October, 1959), p. 1.

[7] For technical treatment of this subject, see Milton Friedman and Anna J. Schwartz, *A Monetary History of the United States 1867–1960* (Princeton, N.J., Princeton University Press, 1963), and Friedman, "The Demand for Money: Theoretical and Empirical Results," *Journal of Political Economy*, vol. 67 (August, 1959), pp. 327-51. For easier reading, see Milton Friedman, *Capitalism and Freedom* (Chicago, University of Chicago Press, 1962), Chapter III. For an explanation and declaration of Friedman's victory, see Albert L. Kraus, "Is Keynes Defunct?" *The New York Times* (November 6, 1968), p. 53, and "The Debate Over Money Supply," *The Economist* (October 26, 1968), pp. 16-17. Also, Allan H. Meltzer, "Major Issues in the Regulation of Financial Institutions," *Journal of Political Economy* (August, 1967).

such bloody systems, their performance has been poor. Russia's growth rate has been about the same as that of the United States since 1917, and yet she invests twice as much of her gross national product (GNP) in plant and equipment to get this growth (30 percent of Russia's compared with 15 percent of the U.S.'s GNP). Japan invests as much as Russia, but gets more than twice the growth (about 10 percent per year compared to Russia's 3 or 4 percent).[8]

Taxes now take over 30 percent of our GNP, but as Michael Harrington has observed, "the welfare state benefits least those who need help most. . . ."[9] In fact, federal, state and local taxes take an astounding 34 percent of the income of those who make less than $3,000 a year.[10]

Minimum wage laws increase unemployment and especially hurt the poor.[11] If a person can only produce

[8] Professor G. Warren Nutter, *The Growth of Industrial Production in the Soviet Union* and "The Structure and Growth of Soviet Industry: A Comparison with the United States," *Journal of Law and Economics*, vol. II (October, 1959), pp. 147-74. "How Well Off Are the American and Soviet Consumers?" *Road Maps of Industry*, No. 1607, National Industrial Conference Board (December 1, 1968): "Although the level of welfare of the average Soviet citizen has improved markedly in recent years, it has not gained relative to that of his counterpart in the U.S." Also see my "The Failure of the Soviet Economy," *The New Guard* (November, 1967), pp. 10-12.

[9] *The Other America* (Baltimore, Penguin, 1962), p. 16. ". . . the welfare state . . . helped the poor least of all. Laws like unemployment compensation, the Wagner Act, the various farm programs, all these were designed for the middle third in the cities, for the organized workers, and for the upper third in the country, for the big market farmers. If a man works in an extremely low-paying job, he may not even be covered by social security or other welfare programs."

[10] *U.S. News & World Report* (December 9, 1968).

[11] Professor Yale Brozen, "The Untruth of the Obvious: The Failure of Government Economic Intervention," *The Freeman* (June, 1968). In 1948 the minimum wage was

a dollar's worth of output in an hour (because of poor training or whatever), no one is going to pay him $1.60 an hour (the current federal minimum wage). He will either be unemployed or find a job not covered by the law.

Welfare is now widely recognized as a failure.[12] Farm subsidies have benefited the rich farmer but not the poor.[13] Labor unions use their government-protected monopoly powers to exclude poor and minority workers. Millions of poor have been thrown out of their homes by urban renewal, so they have to crowd into fewer, higher-rent apartments.[14] Licensing requirements keep the poor out of a multitude of jobs from taxi drivers to beauty operators to CPA's.

We must now take a new direction. We should expand *personal* freedom by abolishing the draft, censorship and all laws that regulate or restrict pot, acid, narcotics, alcohol, cigarettes, gambling, contraception, abortion, prostitution, cohabitation or any act that does

---

40 cents an hour and both white and nonwhite male teenagers' unemployment was about 10 percent. The rate rose to $1.25 by 1963 and white unemployment increased to 16 percent and nonwhite to 27 percent, in a time of record prosperity. See *Manpower Report of the President*, 1967, pp. 203-4, 216. See also Professor James Tobin, "Improving the Economic Status of the Negro," *Daedalus* (Fall, 1965), pp. 889-90.

[12] Hubert Humphrey, *U.S. News & World Report* (May 27, 1968). ". . . one thing I'm positive of: the present system of welfare has out-lived its ultimate usefulness. In fact, it's regressive. We've got to find some better way. . . ."

[13] Richard Cornuelle, *Reclaiming the American Dream*, p. 16. "Eighty per cent of the commodity subsidies now go to one million farmers whose average income exceeds $9,500 while the other 20 per cent is spread thinly among the remaining two-and-a-half million poor farmers."

[14] Professor Martin Anderson, *The Federal Bulldozer*, (Cambridge, Massachusetts Institute of Technology, 1965), pp. 220-21.

not violate the property rights of others.[15] In other words, our bodies belong to us and we alone should decide what we do with them. Some will surely do foolish things, but we have the right only to advise (not force) them to do otherwise. Reality punishes error far more effectively than do legislatures and police. "If you protect every man from his folly, you will raise a nation of fools."

Members of my generation who have turned on with psychedelic chemicals are specially aware of the insanity and tyranny of government. They know from their own experiences that there is little harm in the use of these drugs. Many realize that if man is going to be able to enjoy, even just cope with the fantastically complex society and world of the future, he will have to have the help of mind-expanding drugs.

Authoritarianism assumes (1) that we *know* how everyone should live, and (2) that we have the right to *force* them to live that way. The libertarian denies both. If man is to progress, some must try new ways. Many will fail. But we will all gain from those who find better ways.

Human progress requires both personal and economic freedom. If you regulate and tax the entrepreneur, you reduce his freedom and incentive to provide the ever increasing goods and services, comforts and necessities that we all enjoy. The growth rate of the United States has steadily fallen with the rise of statism. All of our hopes and dreams depend upon our continued economic expansion. Yet big brother can bring it all to an end. We are struck, therefore, by the irony that the hippy and the businessman have a common interest—freedom. When they stop trying to impose

[15] This would put the mafia out of business, or rather into legitimate business, i.e., this would end organized crime which thrives on "morality" laws.

their respective fascisms on each other and work together for both personal and economic freedom, the
millennium will be near.

To expand *economic* freedom it would be ideal to
reduce government to the minimum and end taxation
and regulation. Unfortunately, this ideal may be a long
way off. But we should begin moving in that direction.
To start we can adopt several programs.

Today we have a vast bureaucracy; we spend from
$50 billion to $100 billion a year on programs that are
supposed to help the poor, but little gets to them. The
federal government should end its involvement in welfare; free enterprise, voluntary charitable organizations
and local government should be encouraged to solve
the problems of the poor.[16] Then the federal government, or better still, the states, should enact a negative
income tax that would give poor families some percentage (say 25 percent) of the difference between
what they earn and some base amount (say $6,000 for
a family of four).[17]

There would be several advantages to this approach:
(1) it would be cheaper for taxpayers; (2) it would
probably give more to the poor; (3) it would eliminate
the need for the vast bureaucracy and the horde of
social workers who snoop into the lives of their clients;
(4) it would give more freedom to the recipient to

[16] See Richard Cornuelle, *Reclaiming the American Dream*
(New York, Random House, 1965) and Cornuelle and Robert H. Finch, *The New Conservative-Liberal Manifesto* (San
Diego, Viewpoint, 1968) for an excellent presentation of the
accomplishments and potentialities of the independent sector, i.e., private charities and other nonprofit groups.

[17] Of several articles on the Negative Income Tax among
the best are Milton Friedman, *Capitalism and Freedom* and
"The Case for the Negative Income Tax," Symposium on
Guaranteed Income, Chamber of Commerce of the U.S., De-
cember 9, 1966, pp. 29-55, and reprinted in Document 172
(October 1967) U.S. Government Printing Office, pp. 71-81.

spend his money as he sees fit; (5) it would increase incentive over the present system—the negative income tax would let the recipients keep some percentage of anything they should earn instead of deducting it all as is now done; (6) the program would phase itself out as incomes rise above the base figure; (7) it would not break up families as the present AFDC program does by offering a reward for the father to leave the home.

Students and the poor especially, and more and more other citizens, are becoming increasingly aware of the failure of public education. Paul Goodman wrote in *Compulsory Mis-Education*, "In many under-privileged schools the IQ steadily falls the longer they go to school." [18] Public education has become a state monopoly run by and for the teachers, not the students.

What we desperately need is for the states to stop subsidizing education. If they do subsidize it, they should give the money in voucher checks to parents who will then use the checks to send their children to the school of their choice—public, private or parochial. In order to get students, and especially their money, schools will have to improve. Competition will bring the kind of revolution in education that has occurred in other industries in the private sector such as medicine, transportation, communications and agriculture.

The *only* answer for students trying to improve their college education is for those who donate to colleges (both states and individuals) to give grants to students instead. The students could then pick their college. Good schools would prosper and schools that ignored quality would decline unless they improved. Consumer dollar power is the only way students will ever have a say in improving higher education; certainly not through rioting.

In general, old liberals support personal freedom, but

[18] New York, Random House-Vintage, 1968, p. 26.

not economic; old conservatives support economic freedom, but not personal. Among young people we find a shift toward libertarianism on both sides. The New Left has denounced big government and the liberal establishment in no uncertain terms. The New Right has rejected the neofascism of the Wallace movement.[19] They have joined the New Left to work for abolition of the draft, an increased student voice on campus, a negative income tax and private efforts to help the poor. Thus, as my generation takes power, we can hope to see a movement to a freer society.[20]

The American Revolution is not over.

[19] Young Americans for Freedom with thirty thousand members is the leading conservative youth group in the United States. A poll of their members showed that less than 4 percent supported Wallace (*The New Guard* [October, 1968], p. 3).

[20] Perhaps all young people (certainly young Czechs) can understand Ethan Allen, quoted in Charles A. and Mary R. Beard, *New Basic History of the United States* (New York, Doubleday, 1960):

"Ever since I arrived at the state of manhood and acquainted myself with the general history of mankind, I have felt a sincere passion for liberty. The history of nations doomed to perpetual slavery, in consequenct of yielding up to tyrants their natural-born liberties, I read with a sort of philosophical horror; so that the first systematical and bloody attempt at Lexington, to enslave America, thoroughly electrified my mind, and fully determined me to take part with my country."

Pat Mayweather

Twenty-year-old Miss Mayweather was born in Detroit but grew up in Memphis, Tennessee. At thirteen she joined the NAACP, working in election campaigns, voter registration drives, community action organizations. Now a junior at Mount Holyoke, she is a member of the Afro-American Society but describes her present state of mind as "removed and evaluating."

What is America? For some it's a melting pot of diverse peoples and cultures come together in harmony to form a new race of men. For others America is a terrible nightmare in which men are exploited and deprived of their humanity. Now, after almost two hundred years of living a lie, the people who run America— whoever they are—must deal with the reality of its shortcomings.

We are trying desperately to define the problem and to decide on the quickest possible solution. For such an abstract question we so often look for a solution in material things. Studies are made to define the problem; proposals are written to provide solutions. But what good are they? Ultimately, a building can never solve anything, nor can money or jobs. Perhaps they pacify a violent mob, but they don't get to the heart of the problem. The only things that will do any lasting good are love and mutual understanding. And the effects of these cannot be seen quickly, but must transpire over a long period of time.

Armed with a feeling of desperation and aided by emotional rhetoric, we seek solutions that will allow us to see clearly the steps leading to our goal.

We want freedom *now*, not tomorrow, but *now*!

This familiar chant raises only one question in my mind: What kind of freedom is attainable tomorrow?

Is freedom being able to eat at any restaurant, live in any neighborhood, work at any business establishment, go to any school? Yes, we can have these rights tomorrow, but how can we ever live and work in peace as long as hate and unfounded prejudices continue to eat away at the hearts of men.

We are impatient—we have a right to be after so many years of bondage—but we must not let our desperation cloud our vision and prevent us from seeing where the real problem lies.

We must realize that receiving freedom tomorrow is impossible. This is not to say that we must completely abandon our struggle to get what is rightfully ours; rather, we must realize that the problem does not end with a few victories in the courts. In our personal contact with our brothers, we must try to understand what makes them tick. Only this effort will, in the end, bring lasting freedom.

We are weak; we thrive on each other. The most difficult thing you can ever ask a person to do is stand alone and be a man. Every day we face a dilemma. We must decide how, as individuals, we can maintain and safely exercise honest judgment in an environment in which the surest route to advancement is in conforming to the standards of the people who run America. Very seldom do we feel free enough to express ourselves with complete candor. Rather, we hide under an impenetrable layer of sophistication, not allowing others to probe the depths of our humanity and making no effort to discover this same humanity in them.

We are all creatures of the American dream of justice and equality. Every so often we realize, if only for a brief moment, that the words "justice" and "equality" are still impossible dreams. We realize that we are denied our inalienable rights. We begin to wonder about our responsibilities in a world so devoid of meaning and purpose. Do we try to find an answer? *No!* We accept defeat before the battle begins, and from then on it's merely a game to get through as easily as possible. We care little about understanding people as human beings. Instead they become obstacles in the road, either to be run over or simply kicked aside.

The American problem goes far beyond that of race. What then is "the problem?" As the structure of society becomes more complex and industrialized, the individual citizen somehow gets lost in the mire. Our individuality is sacrificed to the god of a false majority —false because it does not represent the thinking of the greater part of the American population, but rather a small percentage who are powerful enough to control the thinking of an entire nation. At the expense of our manhood, America flaunts its facade of power and national unity.

I seriously question the ability of this powerful "majority" to determine what is best for every member of society. If this "majority" are merely weaklings who not only lack knowledge of what they really believe, but who also would never think of openly dissenting— then of what value are their decisions? These weaklings become puppets of "the man." They don't exist as independent entities coming together and making the best possible decisions, but rather as leaches clinging fast to unfounded principles and ideas. Why should we continue to wear the gaudy cloak of democracy for all the world to see, when we all know what truth lies underneath: the false majority is really the minority power structure in disguise.

But who makes up this false majority? *You!*

Take a long hard look at yourself; there you will find

"the problem" spelled out in capital letters. You are now and always have been afraid to look really closely at yourself. Your facade may appear strong and hard, but your values, your standards and your philosophies are founded on shifting sand. Probing the depths will likely force you to this reality: you know nothing about yourself; you cling fast to your prejudices because you have nothing else in which to believe. The most difficult thing for you is admitting that you have been wrong. You are totaly submerged in guilt because you are subconsciously aware of your problem and you refuse to acknowledge it. You are afraid to stand tall because the prospect of falling is too great. And you don't want to take the risk.

The problem is not money; the problem is not food; the problem is not jobs. The finger of indictment does not point to any one person or to any one race. The problem is *you*! The problem is *me*! The problem is *everyone*!

If it were simply a matter of one, two and three, the problem as I see it would be:

1. We do not know ourselves.

2. We are too damned sophisticated (to use a euphemism for "disgustingly superficial") in our dealings with other people ever to get anywhere near an understanding of human nature.

3. As a result, we are totally invisible to each other as human beings.

What then are the prospects for a new world of positive meaning and value? First, we must gain new vision that will enable us to see how blind we are to each other's humanity and existence. Whites prefer to think of blacks in stereotyped images of brute beasts or happy minstrels; blacks prefer to think of whites as prejudiced and exploiting bastards. The problem is that each is incapable of viewing the other as *people*.

Secondly, we must seek to assert our individuality in the face of a growing sense of isolation. In the mass, the isolated and the alienated are capable of consent or indifference to extermination camps, napalm bombs and nuclear holocaust. We must realize that humanity is invisible to most persons, black as well as white, and we must seek to discover, each of us for ourselves, what the other thinks, and feels and is.

Finally, we must realize that respect commands itself, and it can *never* be withheld when it is due. By demanding respect for our humanity we begin to respect ourselves. In probing the deepest recesses of self, we discover the mysteries of humanity; the demand for recognition follows naturally.

The Revolution desperately needs thinking men and women. Equipped with a knowledge of self and a basic understanding of what's going on around us, we can do beautiful things toward helping America get together.

We must first choose to work in some phase of the Movement (SDS, Afro-American Society, NAACP—it doesn't really matter which, they all have something to offer), remembering, however, that whenever we join any organization or associate with any group, we automatically sacrifice a certain amount of our individuality and assume the group characteristics to a certain extent.

But we must not be swallowed up by Movement ideology. Rather, we must strive to shape the ideology of the Movement by voicing clear, well-thought-out and honest opinions. If enough of us will do this, then the minority who control America will realize that we will not let them tamper with our minds any longer; we will settle for nothing less than complete respect. As individuals. As *people*!

A new generation has emerged—a generation that is trying desperately to free itself of all the enslaving aspects of American society. We are trying to break away from and denounce "the system" and "the man." Society has become a nightmare. The Founding Fathers are lying in their graves watching their famous words turn to ashes. Some people seem to feel that something terrible is taking place, when actually we are simply trying to make America what it should be. We are beginning to wake up to America as it is, and we will not live such a farce.

We, the new generation, refuse to let you—the blind and brainwashed—enslave us. As Eldridge Cleaver said, "We shall have our manhood. We shall have it or the earth will be leveled by our attempts to gain it."

Nancy McWilliams

Nancy McWillaims is a doctoral candidate in psychology at the City University of New York. Now twenty-three, she grew up in various suburbs of Springfield, Massachusetts, New York City, and Reading, Pennsylvania. At Oberlin College she majored in political science and took part in assorted student crusades on and off campus. For the past two summers she has directed a camp for seven- to twelve-year-old children of widely varied ethnic and economic backgrounds. She owes her early radicalization to her "family, Peter Seeger, Meg Fardy, and her husband Carey."

✠✠✠✠✠✠✠✠✠✠✠✠✠✠✠✠✠✠✠✠✠✠✠✠✠✠✠✠✠✠✠✠✠✠✠✠✠✠✠

"To have great love, you got to have great anger."

"Activism" has become a dirty word lately, and what a shameful thing this is in a country where active, public struggle for social progress has always been a major value. Political involvement by the young is healthy and commendable; those who prefer peace and quiet to a troublesome moral challenge, and hence subscribe to the theory that one's student years are best spent docilely in preparation for the "real world," should read no further. Though it is obviously true, I nevertheless find it incredible that American society regards panty raids, brutal hazing and pointless pranks as more "wholesome" outlets for youthful energy than political activism. Why is activity verging on violence proper when it concerns trivia, and improper when it forces hard questions into public consideration?

Most people today ask in puzzlement or anger why students disrupt the university and rage against American society, the implied assumption being that they could instead be taking advantage of all these offer. But real education simply does not happen to the patient and the passive, and what the university and society offer these days to students seeking genuine learning and moral growth is, in fact, of rather dubious quality. Spokesmen for the student movement have always been very clear on this.[1] Moral outrage is only the other side of what used to be called "youthful enthusiasm" or "the idealism of the young," and since we no longer live in a time when the objects of enthusiasm are obvious or when *idealism* has any clear *ideas,* outrage is by far the saner emotion. The time to worry about students is when they are *not* yelling, or when the objects of their criticism are either sadly petty or hopelessly immune to their influence. Such is now the case.

Students in recent years have lapsed into discouragement about the prospects of activism, an attitude reflected in the peculiarly frantic quality of some of their demands. The implications for American society are ominous to say the least. There are two ways to respond to a world of injustice. One is politically, by struggling in the muck of it all to *do* something, with the risk—or perhaps the inevitability—of getting dirty in the process. This is the response that we Americans, with our diatribes against apathy, have always esteemed. The other is to seek innocence somehow, avoiding involvement lest one be soiled. When those of us with all the spiritual energy of youth respond to social problems with a search for personal innocence, our alienation is due not to fatigue (as it frequently is among our elders), but to the intolerability of the political alternatives. When sense of self is rather new and the

[1] The best source on the philosophical origins of the student movement is M. Cohen and D. Hale, eds., *The New Student Left: An Anthology* (Boston, Beacon Press, 1967).

risks of commitment high, one protects one's personality from possible contamination. If the cause for which one might sell one's soul looks enough like the devil, one opts out of the market: to avoid selling *out*, one does not sell at all. And it is a tragedy, especially in a society so youth-conscious, to have allowed a situation in which the young are prematurely defeated.

Fortunately, awareness of the moral imperative of activism is rooted too deeply in American culture for people of student age to withdraw in good conscience. Ideas of the importance of participation in society, of good citizenship, responsible leadership and conscientious following, of reflection, critical judgment and consequent action, are convictions that were carved into our hearts long before our high school civics teacher taught us How a Bill Becomes a Law, too long ago for the clumsily imported mysticisms of the East to dwell easily in our minds for very long.[2] Hence, succumbing to the temptation to abandon society must be rationalized in the language of activism to be admissible.

The politics of risk and commitment began to be replaced not long ago by the politics of personal purity. Since opting out with scarcely a whimper was too obviously a moral evasion, the young chose to opt out with a political bang. Demonstrations for peace in Vietnam, hunger strikes in sympathy with Biafra, epithets hurled at cops and hysteria about the CIA were not so much attempts to influence policy as high-pitched protestations that *I* have nothing to do with a given evil. It seemed to be all we could do; by an almost

---

[2] Fads embracing one Eastern religion or another are periodic in America, but they come and go rapidly and have never seriously threatened our established Western churches, witness the fleeting popularity of Zen Buddhism and Taoism in the 1950s and the short reign of the erstwhile Maharishi. One wonders, however, if the current rage for sensitivity training will replace them as a more permanent escape mechanism.

ritual "confrontation" we sought personal absolution from evils that looked unconfrontable.

It is easy to see why antipoliticality in the guise of politics became the fashion. The blissful days when a student could go to the South quite unashamed of his liberalism to stand up against a perfectly blatant injustice are gone, complicated by their own by-product, the emergence of a scrappy black dignity. And the situation in Vietnam was hardly a good substitute at which to direct righteous indignation: it was too distant and inaccessible, too complex for accusations of simple racism, too obscured by top-level secrecies and too removed from personal daily life except in the form of a constant, compelling, terrifying threat from one's draft board. The war in Vietnam was a disaster if only for its effects on American young people: we learned the dangerous lesson of helplessness. And so the weakly convincing defiance in Phil Ochs's "I Ain't Marchin' Anymore" replaced the power and conviction in "We Shall Overcome."

Political alienation can take one of two forms: passive negativism toward conventional values, or active destruction, usually in the name of some apocalyptic vision. Students, for example, can choose either to escape into drugs, surfboards, the promise of suburban wife-swapping and similar palliatives, or set a few bombs. Both alternatives reflect the conviction that standard political channels, if not hopelessly clogged, lead only to the eventual abandonment of one's goals. Both are pathetic and wasteful.

The politics of purity, whether passive or aggressive, is the logical result of accelerating technological change and the increasing complexity of life. If things have gotten so bad—and I think they have—that the search for innocence as a political style is inevitable, the destructive response is far preferable to passive withdrawal. In the first place, action, even "senseless" violence, at least forces Americans to recognize that despite an abundance of electric can-openers and moon-shots something has gone drastically wrong in the society—something they might manage to overlook if they all simply turned on and dropped out quietly. Second, activism necessarily includes the possibility of political education: by battling the system one can learn something about what kinds of battles get what kinds of results. Unfortunately, the signs are that it is already too late; political activity on campus these days is largely confined to blacks, with only secondary involvement by others.

Nevertheless, political leaders who are truly concerned about the politics of purity, active or passive, can at least stall off further alienation if only they will listen between the lines to what young people are saying. For example: The desire for *community* pervades the thought of every current youth movement, from the hippy love cults to SDS's ideal of participatory democracy to the wishful assertations of blacks that they are all somehow brothers. One might consider this the wish to return to the emotional security of the home town, except that, in fact, few in my generation have *had* home towns, at least not the organically functioning communities or neighborhoods our parents knew as children. We have had either the suburb—a sprawling, aimless, mindless leach on some troubled city—or the city itself—a place of confusion and fear.

Most of us did not even have the comfort of staying in one place; my family, for instance, has lived in seven different houses in four different suburbs since my birth. Under such circumstances, to get even an idea of *where* power lies, not to mention a sense that one *has* some, is a real feat. The ghetto child, helpless against a cumbersome city bureaucracy, finds it virtually impossible. Just as the quest for community reveals a deep need for the basic experience of civic interdependence, the desire for purity of action reflects utter inexperience in acting confidently and proudly in everyday local matters.

Public men in America must deal with both my generation, full of bright and sensitive kids now drifting toward complete estrangement or diffuse and violent anger, and those younger people, including the yet unborn, who deserve an inheritance better than cynicism. This means straining not only resources but —more important—*imaginations* to provide more options to those of student age, new and various ways to contribute to the furthering of our common values. It also means creating the kind of society that will respond to the strivings of our children with something better than an automated shrug.

As to the problem of those of us now in our teens and twenties, the successes of the Peace Corps and Vista testify to some possibilities; combined, these programs deal with only the smallest fraction of desperately wanting areas of service. Why not attack several problems at once, including the sticky question of the draft, by requiring, for example, two years of service from every American, to come sometime between, say, ages fifteen and thirty, in which enlistment in the armed forces is only one of many options.[3] I can think of scores of jobs that might be included: custodial or assistantship work in hospitals and schools; all kinds of teaching; programs to assist the elderly, disabled and bedridden; forestry and conservation jobs; child

[3] Draft reforms along these lines have been suggested by several people, including Sargent Shriver. Hopefully by the time this manifesto is published, some of the proposed plans will have received more than a cursory nod for inventiveness.

supervision for working mothers; manual work on public projects; community organization. . . .

The more flexible the system, the better. Optimally,
people would be given their first- or second-choice service, there would be provision for serving in separate
areas during different years, service years could be
taken discontinuously, work over a specified number
of summers would also qualify, there would be provision for applicants who wish to work with an approved
private service agency, etc. In modern America such a
plan could mitigate the much (deservedly) touted
abuses of present notions of "service," e.g., the military, which affects only males (predominantly those of
lower income), and only those who are considered
healthy and upright, according to whatever notions of
health and integrity a local draft board finds most ad-
vantageous. As long as we are stuck with computers,
let's put them to work for a change in the service of
honoring diversity of choice instead of mandating
bureaucratic rigidity.

Similarly, we should use the media to publicize some
ignored good causes, for the decent parts of the
American soul respond pretty well when battered with
evidence of waste and injustice. We could use a care-
ful look at many situations *before* they reach the crisis
point for once. Here, in random order, are some of my
nominations for public issues:

Now that organ transplants are virtually the order
of the day, who will determine who is the heart
"donor" (a grotesque euphemism) and who the recipient? Will the market regulate it as always before,
with the result that the poor die literally to supply the
blood of the wealthy?

How shall we regulate forthcoming intelligence- and
personality-manipulating chemicals?

Why is the suicide rate in America rising swiftly? And why especially among the young?

What shall we do about increasing corporate concentration? How can such power centers be kept from getting even more distant from the people?

What about the coming "moneyless" society, when a few giant banks punch our shifting credits and debits on and off distant cardboard strips? Will the poor have credit cards too?

How shall we hold foundations to account? How can they be prevented from promoting inequality by dodging taxes? [4]

Why do most millionaries still pay only a pittance to society?

What is happening to the small farmer? Why are his children leaving the land, depriving us not only of our most efficient food producers, but also of our symbol of all the old American virtues? Why are those virtues no longer paying off for him?

How shall we preserve the identity of special subcommunities like the Amish, who perceived the perils of technology long before the rest of us?

The list could go on and on.

New service areas and new muckraking are badly needed, but at best they are temporizing gestures, stopgap attempts to wave off the steam of a boiling pot still sitting on high heat. In order to "bring the children home," as wishful thinkers hoped the McCarthy campaign had done, it remains to make home tolerable.

[4] For example, the Center for the Study of Democratic Institutions publishes tax-free a glossy magazine of comment that effectively competes with the major privately-owned liberal magazines that struggle to make ends meet. For a brilliantly unsympathetic look at the Center, see Joan Didion, *Slouching Towards Bethlehem* (New York, Farrar, Straus & Giroux, 1968), the chapter called "California Dreaming."

American society is not now tolerable for the cream of its own youth, for exactly the reasons we keep vainly shouting: it is too big, anonymous, inaccessible and morally impoverished. It responds to our shouts by trying to buy us off—New Leftists write for *Look* and Madison Avenue transforms the hippy protest into high fashion—and it is rich enough that we are afraid we'll sell, ending up in some guilt-ridden Scarsdale where our children will be even greater strangers to communality than we were.

To get at the fire under the pot we must reestablish in America the conditions for real homes, communities whose centers lie within their own borders and not eighty minutes away on the 7:28 train. Tocqueville said that one reason democracy could work in America was that in the small New England towns, which were its guts, people could feel some *personal* stake in the system: their participation made some difference and their positions had some dignity. I was lucky enough for awhile to go to a small high school in an area where population was pretty stable and where students consequently knew their teachers and each other well enough to feel some personal stake in the community. Most of us were also able to find some area of competence in which to win recognition; through academics, athletics or social and political involvement we learned that the "system" in our town did respond to us. (We did not call it a system, of course, since we were on intimate terms with it, quite unlike the relationship between today's average student and the mammoth university, school system or society he faces.) I know now from comparing my secondary education to that of friends from big, efficient suburban high schools that we paid a certain academic price for our parochialism, but we also knew we were human beings.

Surely our cultural sentimentality for the frontier, our delight at Hal Holbrook as Mark Twain, our appreciation of nostalgic books like Willie Morris's *North Toward Home*, and our exasperation at the "rat race" betray a deep suspicion that the clerk at the old General Store had a more satisfying life than today's nine-to-five junior executive, in spite of his electric lawnmower. But almost no one is talking publicly about how to create analogous human conditions in this age of technology. The right wing picks out scattered symptoms and yelps to go back to a pre-income tax Golden Age that never existed. Liberals, reluctantly noticing the turbulence of a time when living has become so complex, frustrating and tedious that we are all close to explosion, offer only mumbled clichés about "rational discourse" or "compromise" or that old ritual copout "On the one hand . . . on the other hand. . . ." At its best, liberalism tries to deal with fundamental conflicts by a kind of Erich Frommian word magic, insisting that by simply *recognizing* our brotherhood, or our unique individualities, or by being "honest" with one another, or loving, or some such thing, we can leap right over all those nasty problems of societal massiveness, anonymity and unbearably swift change.

We must deal with social problems by legislation more imaginative than appropriations for superhighways, which create short-term efficiency at the price of long-term rootlessness, and make suburbia possible even further from the city (whose poor we rarely see and cannot identify as our own, whose callousness trains us not to notice filth and suffering, whose gritty air makes us forget that cities can be beautiful). Industries must be given incentives to move out of the megapolis—certainly possible in these days when efficient transportation has removed their original reason for locating there—to places where they can be focal points of smaller, prouder towns that would reward the activism of their young with some responsiveness. We must find ways to use public power to reverse those currents that daily make us feel tinier, lonelier, more helpless and more hopelessly resigned or angry.

We have the money to do this; a lot of it goes hurtling to the moon, for no purpose except as a kind of international football game ("Wait till the Russians see *this* play!"). We have the talent too; a lot of it has nowhere to go now but to the streets, or to crowded, smoky, postered rooms where the similarly discouraged know at least the joy of each other's company. Many of us even have the will—those who have not yet forsaken politics for a pseudoinnocence, those who would still like to be able to sing "America the Beautiful" with more pride than embarrassment. The only resource we lack, in fact, is time.

Anne Story Miner

Twenty-nine-year-old Anne Miner "has been female for as long as I can remember." Raised in Evanston, Illinois, and a graduate of both Radcliffe College and Alamoosook Island Camp, Miss Miner moved to California in 1962, where she studied medicine briefly, worked in psychiatric research, published a tract on how to live cheaply in Palo Alto and directed operations for a now-defunct corporation specializing in technical translations. She joined the administrative staff of Stanford University in 1967, where she now works with alumni and students. Miss Miner buys a cord of firewood every year, has a dog named Sheba and is a Scorpio polarized in Leo.

❦❦❦❦❦❦❦❦❦❦❦❦❦❦❦❦❦❦❦❦❦❦❦❦❦❦❦❦❦❦❦❦❦❦❦❦❦

Last year seven girls in the Palo Alto High School and Junior High School Women's Liberation group asked their history teacher to cut out his ho-ho treatment of the suffragette movement. He couldn't understand why they called him a chauvinist and told them that their request for the presentation of admirable women models in literature and history signaled incipient lesbianism. Taking one girl aside, he advised on the sly that she read *Portnoy's Complaint* so that she would see the horrible consequences of "aggressive" women.

In New York a fourteen-year-old high school student went to court to gain admittance to all-male Stuyvesant High School because, in her words,

Aside from being discouraged to study for a career, women are discouraged from preparing for jobs involving anything *but* secretarial work, beauty care, nursing, cooking, and the fashion industry. . . . The girls are taught to be beauticians, secretaries, or health aides. This means that if a girl is seeking entrance to a vocational school, she is pressured to feel that certain jobs are masculine and others feminine. She is forced to conform to the Board of Education's image of her sex. . . . Female students share the general oppressive conditions forced upon everyone by the System's schools, plus a special psychological discrimination showed to women by the schools, the teachers, *and* their fellow students. So, since I don't want *my* issues to get swallowed up in the supposed "larger" issues, I'm going to make women's liberation the center of my fight.[1]

The usual response from both men and women to these girls is that they will fortunately grow up into true womanhood and stop saying things like that. Perhaps it's a self-fulfilling prophecy, but in any case it's still accurate, despite the rash of articles and books on the "sex role issue."

From 1962 to 1966 Stanford undergraduate women confided over and over again to interviewers in a study of college students that they worried about their intelligence and their vitality.[2] Some of them entered college hoping to becoming politicians, scientists or lawyers, as well as wives and mothers, but ended up fearing that their own liveliness, ambition and talent for solving problems was de-sexing them. They wondered if they shouldn't be more passive. A bizarre scene: some of the most talented and fortunate young

[1] Alice De Rivera, "Jumping the Track," from *Leviathan*, vol. 1 (June 1969), p. 17.
[2] Marjorie Lozoff, "Autonomy and the Feminine Role," unpublished monograph (Stanford, California, Institute for the Study of Human Problems, Stanford University, 1968).

people in the country aspiring to an image of pale inadequacy in order to keep their sexual identity.

Marjorie Lozoff, one of the interviewers, recalls how she gave long thought to the tangled question of virtues for men and women. One day she discovered the startling truth: If intelligence, a sense of personal worth, autonomy and a desire to test one's capabilities are virtues, they are human virtues. Not male virtues. By the same token, of course, compassion, the ability to nurture and be nurtured, and openness to one's own and others' feelings are human virtues. Not female virtues. And something's very wrong when a young person must risk a kind of sexual suicide if he or she aspires to any one of these. The male who must deny his interest in children loses as much as the female who never develops her talent for leadership.

But isn't everything getting better? After all, isn't Yale going coed?

"O breathless season," as Mary Ellman puts it, "when Yale shudders like a peacock on the edge of coeducation." [3] Breathless indeed, in view of the fact that Yale can't really go coed—Yale can only admit women into itself, an institution shaped to meet the needs and values of young, white, upper-class males.

Imagine a university that makes sense for both sexes: Graduate fellowships that routinely include childcare expenses as a normal human need. Women professors who do not regard themselves as "lucky," but who people all ranks of the faculty and provide models of competence for young women. Compensatory training for the male professors who cannot see women as their successors as scholars. Part-time degree programs that allow people with young children to be students and parents simultaneously. Recruitment of talented ma-

[3] Mary Ellman, "In America, the Great Brain Divide," *Vogue* (May, 1969), p. 152.

ture women who offer a unique perspective, but who normally suffer from the same lack of self-confidence that afflicts some members of ethnic minorities. Day-care centers staffed by both men and women. A proportionate number of female trustees. Imagine that.

In a way, imagine what you want. The structure of any public institution designed to serve the current life pattern and the full interests of American women can't be described. We haven't seen one yet. The task of designing and advocating such institutions is what we have yet to do.

As long as our institutions continue to reflect the current interests, skills and values of white upper- and middle-class males, "equal opportunity" in America will mean opportunity only for the brightest and most determined black, Indian, Chicano, poor male and any-class female. Expecting things to "get better" with anything short of elimination of institutional discrimination is about as promising as eliminating racism through brotherhood commercials. The problem springs from values and beliefs, but the solution is to build structures that allow people from diverse groups to grow, to think, to love, to test their own capacity for achievement, and to be rewarded for doing so.

What is institutional discrimination?

You are a forty-year-old woman with children. You like graphic design. You'd like to receive public value (money) for your talents in that area. You apply for a job in an advertising firm. The personnel officer tells you (with a straight face) that women aren't hired in professional training programs, that you can start as a typist, and if you are lucky, work yourself up to a professional job. This is institutional discrimination. It does not occur to you to point out that this approach is not only lunatic, it's illegal. That would be unwomanly.

Or you are a thirty-year-old woman with two children, and precisely because you enjoy the nurturing role, you wish to work half-time until you are forty and they leave home. God having apparently decreed that professional work requires forty hours a week, you can find no institution that *systematically* provides for career development on a part-time basis.

Mother of three, you work as a secretary. Ready and willing to embrace the traditional nurturing role, you're asked to pay a special price for it. You can't deduct the cost of baby-sitters from your income tax as a cost of employment, nor can you find any government childcare centers. Childcare is not a normal human expense, it is a female expense.

You are a woman graduate student. The college rules specify that if your husband is a student, and you are working, the two of you can live in university housing. If you are a student, and he works, the pair of you can't. Part-time study? Don't be silly. That would dilute the value of the field.

Having just graduated from high school, you shyly apply for a job. Typing skill being a sex-linked genetic characteristic, you are naturally invited to be a secretary. You are not invited into the sales training program because . . . well, you won't stay long (how many men do?) . . . well, then, because you are . . . well . . . a *woman.*

You are pregnant with your fourth child. Because you and your husband both work to provide enough money for the three you have already, you would need a pregnancy leave from your job as well as minimal sustaining pay while you satisfied the traditionally feminine desire to remain at home for the first three months after the baby's birth. But there is no *automatic* provision for the two undeniable facts that married women work and married women have babies.

You are pregnant with your fourth child, which will put an intolerable burden on the family finances and will limit the active participation in local government that you feel is essential to doing a good job as a mother. Your nation, which cannot bring itself to require compulsory gun registration, does not hesitate to demand your compulsory pregnancy.

Middle- and upper-class women can afford to view this kind of discrimination with patience, but for the majority of working women it has severe economic consequences:

> In an average month in 1962, there were 23 million women at work, of whom 17 million were full-time workers. Most of the jobs that women hold are in low-pay categories. In 1960, for example, there were 7 million women clerical workers and only 431 geologists. In 1961, the earnings of women working full-time averaged only about 60 percent of those of men working full-time: women are paid less for the same work. Studies made in 1960 showed area averages of women bank-tellers with less than five years of experience running typically $5-$15 a week less than the averages of men with the same years of experience. Differences ranged from 9 to 49 cents an hour between the averages of men and women in the same power laundry occupations in a number of metropolitan areas.[4]

Other aspects of the economic exploitation of women and discrimination against them must be cited: Negro women constitute the largest minority in the United States, and are the lowest paid and

[4] "American Women," in *The Report of the President's Commission on the Status of Women and Other Publications of the Commission* (New York, Charles Scribner's Sons, 1965).

the most disadvantaged group in the labor force. The median annual wage of white women is less than that of black men. In 1960, nonwhite males earned $3,075; white females, $2,537. Lowest of all are the nonwhite females: $1,276. Yet the black woman often earns more than her husband, and sometimes is the only wage earner in the family.[5]

And it isn't getting any better. Mary Keyserling, former director of the Women's Bureau, notes that "occupationally, women are relatively more disadvantaged today than they were twenty-five years ago." [6] For years the federal government has issued statistics supporting this thesis; Carolyn Bird, in *Born Female*, indisputably documents the economic discrimination against women.

Many people pause at this point, then dive into the biological or historical bases for women not *wanting* more responsibility, freedom, self-respect, autonomy, strength or any of the other values we reward with public esteem, open authority and salaries. But the question is not so much, how did things get this way, but rather, why do we, as women, let them stay this way?

One of the stereotypes of women is that we are helpers. As secretary to the company president or as wife to our husband, we are the comforters and the facilitators. We organize as mothers to help children by improving schools. We organize for housing or for religion. We organize—but always on someone else's behalf. One of the saddest aspects of the feminine

[5] Esther Peterson, "Working Women," in *The Women in America* (Boston, Houghton Mifflin Company, 1965), as cited by Marlene Dixon in "The Restless Eagles," *Motive*, vol. XXIX, (March-April, 1969).

[6] Jo Freeman, "The New Feminists," *The Nation* (February 24, 1969), p. 241.

image we subscribe to is that there is something "un-feminine" about directly and openly working on behalf of other women, and ourselves.

That, of course, is precisely what the suffragettes did, and precisely why the young Palo Alto girls resented a teacher's dismissal of these women as giddy and peculiar ladies.

The young girls' demands are reminiscent of the black demand for Black Studies departments in schools and colleges, and the resemblance is not superficial. For many of the characteristics we now think of as sexual characteristics are simply low-status characteristics. The comparison of female Americans with the old image of black male Americans, for example, is instructive.

Castelike Status of Women and Negroes

Negroes	Women

1. High Social Visibility

| a. skin color, other "racial characteristics | a. secondary sex characteristics |
| b. (sometimes) distinctive dress (and manners)* | b. distinctive dress (special codes of etiquette)* |

2. Ascribed Attributes

| a. inferior intelligence, smaller, less convoluted brain, scarcity of genius | a. ditto |
| b. freer in instinctual gratification, more emotional, "primitive" and childlike, imagined sexual prowess that is envied | b. irresponsible, inconsistent, emotionally unstable, lacking strong superego, image as temptresses (more intuitive, irrational)* |

c. common stereotype
—"inferior"

c. "weaker (women as incomplete men)*

3. Rationalization of Status

a. thought all right in his place
b. myth of contented negro

a. woman's place is in the home
b. myth of contented woman—"feminine" woman is happy in subordinate role

4. Discrimination

a. limitations on education, should fit "place" in society
b. confined to traditional jobs, barred from supervisory positions
c. deprived of political importance
d. social and professional segregation
e. more vulnerable to criticism

a. ditto

b. ditto

c. ditto

d. ditto

e. ditto

5. Accommodation Attitudes

a. supplicatory whining intonation of voice

b. deferential manner
c. concealment of real feelings
d. outwit "white folks"

a. rising inflection, smiles, laughs, downward glances

b. flattering manner
c. "feminine wiles"

d. outwit "menfolk"

e. careful study of points at which dominant group is susceptible to influence	e. ditto
f. fake appeals for directives, show of ignorance	f. appearance of helplessness

The characteristics in parenthesis followed by an asterisk were added by Marlene Dixon.[7]

The comparison is not trivial. The concept of institutional discrimination was first developed by blacks, and the black revolution has inspired and provided models for other "invisible" Americans in the last few years. So although the problems are by no means identical, the new feminist movement will at first resemble ethnic minority movements of the sixties. Women who work for change will disagree about whether to work for "integration" into a male-dominated power structure, or for "separatism"—either in the sense of "Women for Peace" movements or all-female communes. Women who have adapted to the status quo, like middle-class blacks in the early 1960s, will feel very uncomfortable when other women express their forthright anger.

The New Left will argue that women's liberation can come only after the success of the male-lead "revolution," citing Marx' and Engels' remarks on the oppression of women as capitalism's inevitable consequence, while middle-class women picket companies because they have no female executives. Male leaders will naively argue that the "problems" of poverty and racism are more pressing than institutional discrimination against women, and in so doing, display unintended chauvinism by forgetting that half of all the poor people and half of all ethnic minorities suffer from discrimination based on their sex.

[7] Helen Hacker, "Women as a Minority Group," *Social Forces*, vol. 30, p. 65, as cited by Dixon, *op. cit.*

At first, familiar surface changes may occur. More female comics, like black and Jewish comics, may appear to deal with conflict through humor. Textbook authors and television writers will try to correct the one-sided image of women by picturing women doctors and an occasional normal woman spaceship captain.

And all of these changes will intertwine unpredictably with our other dramas of ecological suicide, continuing racism, the new mysticism, automation, overpopulation, the "revolution," the revolt of the white-collar worker, and so on.

But at a deeper level, most of us will resist opening more options for women, and those who work for change will face very serious questions. The many women and men who might support childcare centers because they cherish the nuclear family will form only uneasy alliances, if any, with groups of women who seek such centers as the first step toward termination of the institution of marriage. Political assumptions, racism and class values will cause conflict even among concerned women.

Finally, women will face the serious problem of trying to enter the economic and governmental mainstream of national life without assuming its undesirable traits. Can women learn to stand up for themselves, when that is needed, without falling into the inhumanity that seems to come with power? Is the sex-role question really a subtopic of more general societal questions, or is it not more likely that a serious restructuring of society to provide full humanity for women would bring social and economic consequences more profound than we can imagine?

As a nation we have not only failed to correct institutional discrimination against women, we don't even admit it exists. Most women still gain their personal identity from men: we derive our names from our fathers and husbands; in organized religions we pray to an essentially male God as interpreted by men of the cloth; if married, we gain both livelihood and community status through our husband's role. Even our formal language contains the implicit assumption that woman is the "other," the non-neutral being (collectively, human beings are "men," as in "All men are created equal"). Nations (Sweden, Russia, Israel, for example) that have recognized the issues raised here have found the task of "liberating" women to be difficult indeed; absolutely no modern nation has given this issue top priority, and none has successfully solved it.

In this context, can one seriously expect women to provide the *positive* vision of a realistic social organization that would provide diversity by sex at all levels of decision making? Will anyone be able to provide a meaningful vision of the new masculinity and femininity that would allow the expression of the full potential of both sexes?

Whatever the answers, for many the era of innocence is over. If there *is* some "female" principle of love and sensitivity to the inner mystery of humankind, then surely the day has come for this principle, and the sex allegedly most in tune with it, to influence public policy. If, as is more likely, women and men are equally capable and needful of both strength and love, then we have no excuse for continuing to deny participation in public life to the majority of women.

As a nation we must create institutions that make sense. Primarily through the efforts of ethnic groups we *do* know how to begin to reverse institutional discrimination. We know that leisurely review of the situation by those at the top—be they corporation presidents, bishops or college presidents—is not enough. After hundreds of years of learning to "know its place" as a sexual or ethnic caste, no group stands ready in great numbers equipped with the self-confidence, sophistication and skills needed in most positions of responsibility. Reform, in other words, requires the swift, determined investment of resources in recruiting, training, promoting and providing enabling programs for the group heretofore assumed "naturally" incapable of or uninterested in responsibility. These things must be done not because they are "good" to do, but because *not* doing them is participating in a system that inevitably denies options to many citizens.

Ironically, those who claim to value harmony, monogamous marriage and the family will probably do most to harm them. By opposing the changes that appear to upset the old order (automatic childcare, pregnancy leave, part-time executive positions, etc.), these people will be opposing the very changes on which the long-term survival of the nuclear family rests. For if women continue to be denied options on the grounds that for them marriage and childbearing necessarily mean restriction and subservience, many will eventually question the value of a social structure that demands that half the population abandon personal growth and freedom for the sake of the other half.

That the whole effort will involve great uproar, and that many women will oppose "going too fast," or even "equality" itself, should come as no surprise to observers of other social movements. But the effort has already begun.

Betty Friedan and the thousands of women who have joined N.O.W. (National Organization for Women) since its organizing conference in 1965 have formed nationwide chapters to use traditional civil rights techniques to gain fair employment and legal reform.[8]

[8] "Statement of Purpose, N.O.W.," adopted at organizing conference, October 26, 1966, Washington D.C.

On July 8, 1969, four Republican Congresswomen called on President Nixon to discuss women's rights as citizens and as human beings, and to urge elimination of discrimination against women. In spite of our national distaste for the word "feminist," they saw clearly their special responsibility both to other women and to the nation.[9]

The Fair Employment Commission suddenly has to deal with women who take seriously the Civil Rights Act that forbids employment discrimination on the basis of sex.[10]

Women educators who sadly acknowledged that women were lucky to get educated at all now talk seriously about pressing for changes to allow more than token educational opportunities at the graduate and professional levels.[11]

Told more than once that "the only place of women in the Movement is prone," women in the New Left formed into hundreds of small groups and now argue about how "separate" the drive for Women's Liberation should be.[12]

In Los Angeles, the bellwether of America's future, three young women formed the new Union for Women's International Liberation (UWIL) in 1969 and immediately presented ten requests to UCLA's Chancellor Charles E. Young, who accepted four as obvious needs.[13]

W.I.T.C.H. (Women's International Terrorist Conspiracy from Hell) hexed Wall Street as the symbol

[9] Marian Ash, "Skirting the Capitol" (July 23, 1969, Sacramento, California).

[10] Freeman, op. cit., p. 242.

[11] See the Radcliffe Quarterly issue for Fall 1969, for example.

[12] See "Bread and Roses," by Kathy McAfee and Myrna Woods, in Leviathin (June 1969), p. 8, for discussion by New Left women of Women's Liberation.

[13] See USLA Daily Bruin (May 21, 1969).

of "chauvinist" power, and picketed the Miss America Pageant organizers as participants in the economic exploitation of women. Giving college scholarships to the winners does not override the stronger message that woman's highest goal is to be white, virginal, amusingly but not seriously capable, and above all else childish and grateful.

Hearing about such efforts, some men and women display defensive laughter or open anger. Most people express surprise or straightforward doubt about changing the status quo. We must remind them, and ourselves, that it is a question of providing options to half of America's citizens, and the results will benefit both men and women. Some people have long since seen and overcome sexual stereotyping at the personal level. They must now support women's organized efforts to increase the options for women with the same vigor they give to other civil rights efforts.

We can each begin in our own way. Homemakers can refrain both from putting themselves down as "just a housewife," and from scorning women who want meaningful work outside the home. Professional women can question whether being told they "think like a man" is a compliment or an insult and can work to create the training jobs and part-time career positions needed if we are to see any large number of women in the professions in the near future.

Women who have worked in party politics for years can begin to value themselves and other women enough to ask about the dearth of female candidates. And they can pressure legislators for changes in laws that unfairly penalize both men and women on false sexual expectations. (The single policeman in Chicago who had to fight for two years to adopt a child suffers as much as the poor woman who must bear a child against her will.)

Wealthy women can accept their special role and donate to projects and invest in companies that promote opportunities for other women. For although one of our current national methods of attempting to change institutions is by violent confrontation, the most effective American method is still entirely nonviolent. That method is money. Companies rarely change their promotion policy when urged to or asked to, when picketed or sent bundles of telegrams. Corporations invest in the demanding project of promoting and training minorities—be they racial or sexual—when (1) their board of directors commits itself to doing so, (2) somebody pays them to invest in this training, and/or (3) they can't get a contract unless they do. Arguments fade, stereotypes suddenly seem less important—they find a way.

Finally, young parents can consider seriously their role in perpetrating myths that will inevitably harm their own children. In the light of overpopulation, the divorce rate, contraception and increased life expectancy, one surely does a daughter a disservice by teaching her explicitly or implicitly that passivity and incompetence will make her desirable and thus happy forever. Precisely because we love them, we must make sure our daughters do acquire confidence in themselves as full human beings. Gentleness has little value when it springs from fear of appearing "aggressive" or from lack of self-respect, and "feminine" self-effacement is a pathetic form of celebration of sexual differences.

Similarly, one hardly does one's son a favor by teaching him that to express his feelings "like a girl" is cause for shame. A sense of self-worth that rests on the lack of worth of other groups always cripples its possessor. This kind of "strength" is based on a brittle defense against one's own needs. And ultimately it destroys its possessor.

As Erik Erikson says:

There will be many difficulties in a new joint adjustment of the sexes to changing conditions, but they do not justify prejudices which keep half of mankind from participating in planning and decision making, especially at a time when the other half, by its competitive escalation and acceleration of technological progress, has brought us and our children to the gigantic brink on which we live.[14]

[14] Erik Erikson, "The Inner Space," in *Identity, Youth and Crisis* (New York, W. W. Norton & Co., Inc., 1968).

Roger C. Newell

While still a student at Eastern High School in Washington, D.C., Roger Newell helped form The Modern Strivers, a group of young people who established their own Freedom School, raising $100,000 to finance personnel and curriculum for the first accredited student-run Black Studies program in the country. At nineteen, he is now a sophomore at Columbia College in New York.

✠✠✠✠✠✠✠✠✠✠✠✠✠✠✠✠✠✠✠✠✠✠✠✠✠✠✠✠✠✠✠✠✠✠✠✠✠

The time has come for black people to deal with real problems. The movement is in the last stages of the rhetoric revolution, a military composed of mouths with rank earned simply by one's rap.

Black people now view their struggle as a life-or-death venture. There is no place for "weekend warriors" in the struggle for black liberation in this colony. Black men and women know they are not only fighting for their lives, but also for the lives of the coming generations into whose hands the flame will be passed when the battle takes its toll.

These warriors have reached the conclusion that it is not going to be a three-month fight, it is going to be a fight of lifetimes, many lifetimes. For in the minds of black folks there can only be one of two ends to this fight: either there will be total extermination or total liberation. There is no changing, no wait a minute, no I don't want to be involved or I don't have the time, for when it comes down, you're either going to be black or you're going to be white, no ifs, ands or buts. It's going to be kill or be killed. To quote a brother in the street, "the shit has started." And it is going to be a long time before the end is even in sight.

The odds are piled heavy on the side of white people. Their main weapon is systematic genocide, complete and total: starvation of black people, assassination of black leaders, brainwashing of the masses of black people forced to live in contemporary versions of a concentration camp and forced to be dependent on drugs (which are supplied and controlled from outside the colony). With these facts facing us, we are justified in using any means at our disposal to fight back on both the defensive and the offensive.

The battle now is for (1) the minds of black people, (2) the goods and services of the black community, and (3) the mechanisms of force and violence in the black community. To win a total victory one must control all three.

To control the minds of black people we must deal with the forces that shape them: TV, radio, movies, newspapers, schools, etc. To deal with this problem we must divide ourselves into groups. The first group would be the older black folk whose minds have already been destroyed by the system. These people must be taught not to think of themselves as inferior to white people. Then the real work of teaching them pride can begin. Then there is the very young group, open and waiting to hear how beautiful they are.

But there are other important areas of mass communication. For example, many commercials do nothing but make black people feel inferior. One is about a bandage described as "flesh tone," but just imagine a black child using this product and seeing a pink spot (a pink mass representing *flesh*) on her arm. Now imagine the changes that her mind goes through wondering what is wrong with her skin.

We black people face many problems, but none is as important as the complete control of some black people by the racist, inhuman system and society. The minds of the majority of black people are under the control of "the man." This is the most pressing problem blacks must begin to deal with. It faces us every day of our lives, whenever we read a newspaper or listen to the radio. Terms like "moderate" and "militant" are constantly being driven into our minds. Are these terms real? Can they really define the problems of black people in this colony? These words only show the means that are advocated to reach certain ends But let us look at the ends. Are they different for moderates or militants? The answer is no.

We black people must begin to look at conditions in this country. We must also understand that there is no hope to be found in American justice. We cannot expect to use the laws of America to save ourselves. We must be ready to deal with what comes. For example, a case recently came before a judge in Maryland, on the outskirts of Washington, D.C. It concerned a black woman charged with trying to use a knife on her husband. The judge made the following statement: "If they want to live like animals, let them stay in pens." With men such as these, how can the ends of justice be realized? Black people must understand that these are not things that happen once in a while, but rather this is the pattern of all American justice. This is the reason that James Earl Ray was sentenced to life in prison, but a brother, Almend Evans, was sentenced to die in the electric chair.

W. E. B. Du Bois, in *The World and Africa*, tells how the seven lines of human endeavor were used by black people to lay the foundation for civilization as the world knows it today. This is what black people must become involved in now. They must become a part of the creation of a new black life-style for a new Black Nation. At the core of the new nation will be found the new black family. This will be a family that will be living within a black frame of reference. The black male will be at the head of the new family. His word will rule. The black female will be charged with the responsibility of transmitting the culture of black people.

Black people must look around and check out what is happening to them. The fact is, the new identity of black people is being destroyed by some of the same forces that are trying to destroy black people. Black culture is now something sold by the same groups that once sold black people. The idea of "black" has gone into mass production. How valid is the idea of black dress when the same stores that would not give black people credit are now buying all the African prints they can get their hands on? How valid is the idea of natural hair when some of the same wig companies that were trying to tell black women that their hair was ugly are now mass-producing natural Afro wigs? How valid is the idea of a black revolution when Hollywood has already started making money on movies about their version of the black revolution in this country?

The time has come for black people to stand up and begin to create for themselves a world in the middle of this waste that some call America. Black people must make a new life for themselves. Life or death is the question. For the real power in the black community will not be decided by who controls 200,000 votes, but by who controls the 22's, 25's, 38's, 45's and the M-16's.

Lenny Rubenstein

Born in 1944 in Royston, Hertfordshire, England, shortly after a B-17 crashed at a nearby American air base, Mr. Rubenstein was educated in New Jersey public schools, New York University and presently the City University of New York. A self-professed "Hasidic Marxist," he has a seven-inch scar on his upper left arm, a legacy of his present residence on New York's Lower East Side. His publications to date include articles on London and Paris in *Fifth Estate*, research abstracts in *Poverty and Health in the U.S.* and film reviews and reportage for New York's underground newspaper *Rat*.

❖❖❖

Despite the commonly held belief that films are not politically, ideologically or socially biased, every film is as important to any radical struggle for change as the improvements in the armaments of the police departments across the country. Those David Niven–Doris Day epics, or the spear-and-sandal spectacles, or even the James Bond series conveyed political and ideological themes by their distortion of reality, debasement of history and promulgation of stereotypes. In those blissfully inane movies about missing birth-control pills or idiot surfers the hero (heroes abound in this type of film) was never an ordinary mortal with a rotten job that devours forty hours of his life each week. In *Young at Heart* Frank Sinatra does have a job he hates, but he is supported in his attempts at becoming a songwriter by his wife, played by Doris Day. Every domestic crisis evokes a song, even his wife's pregnancy, which occurs when he is unemployed on some snowy night. This film with its rank sentimentality about the poor and promise of a glamorous, successful career as a singer was produced in the 1950s as the cinematic expression of confidence and joy amid the official fears of subversion and the popular craze for hexachlorophene.

If the poor can be shown without poverty, the wealthy are always abstracted from their money. The 1930s films that ignored the realities of the Depression —*Happy Days* (1930), *Grand Hotel* (1932), *Dinner at Eight* (1933) and *Tarzan and His Mate* (1934)—are the predecessors of more recent films about the wealthy jet set. *In the Cool of the Day* features Jane Fonda amid the ruins of the Parthenon, while *Sabrina* focuses on the domestic problem of romance between the wealthy and the working class. By reducing the issue of social class to a foil in a love affair, as in *Sabrina*, or by ignoring the problem completely, most films about the wealthy tastefully avoid those differences that separate the upper class from the anxious middle class and their numbed victims. When the films that most Americans see refuse to depict poverty or degradation, it is little wonder that problems of racism, the war, slums or drugs remain unpleasant, and more importantly, unexplainable issues.

Many people would object to social criticism of all films, but even *Rosemary's Baby* is a fine example of social biases that go undetected by most audiences. In most witchcraft-devil pacts the hero or victim sells *his* soul to Satan for fame or fortune. Marlow's *Doctor Faustus*, Benét's "The Devil and Daniel Webster" and Goethe's *Faust* are the best examples of this approach. In the William Castle production of *Rosemary's Baby* the husband sells *his wife's body* to the devil, an interesting comment on male domination. The wife, superbly played by Mia Farrow, is a sweet thing whose purposes in life are the decoration of their new apartment, wearing expensive clothes and bearing a child that happens to be Satanic. There could not have been a more vicious attack on women's role in contemporary society than this film, although the banalities of some cigarette commercials are equally representative. Even if by consciously excluding issues or problems, all films are images of a society's history and fears.

Historical melodrama is a field in which the big studios constantly display poor taste and atrocious scholarship. Except for the leftist idealism in *Spartacus,* where there are definite hints of international solidarity among Rome's slaves (written in by Dalton Trumbo and Howard Fast), almost every historical film from Hollywood debases history and reduces it to the level of a large fist fight. There used to be a film, *The Black Book,* shown on television almost monthly which reduced the Jacobin period of the French Revolution to the most basic kind of power struggle between Robespierre's fanatics and the more moderate Girondists. The writer and director ignored the facts that would have invalidated their characterization of the Jacobin leader. They did not mention the corruption that existed among the moderate leaders, the war the moderates had started or the excesses they committed after Robespierre's death. Many historians ignored these facts too, especially after Napoleon and the restoration of the monarchy. Unfortunately, the *newer* interpretation (actually it's at least forty years old) has not yet reached Hollywood.

This cultural lag is best illustrated by the moviemakers' image of the Second World War. In most wartime films no effort was made to inform the audience of the reasons for fighting Hitler. The realities of fascism and its roots in modern society were reduced to Gestapo thugs and old-style Prussian officers. Except for the 1939 production *Confessions of a Nazi Spy,* which used real settings and a documentary approach to the problem of military espionage and FBI investigations, most Hollywood war films used fairly gross images and simplistic themes. In *Four Sons*, a 1940 film that tried to depict Sudeten life before and after Hitler, Don Ameche plays the patriotic son who fights it out with his brother, who happens to be a Nazi in SS black. The two die; Ameche's death, while huddled in his mother's arms, is filmed through the boots of a passing German parade. America's entry into the war did not change matters; in 1943, after the battles that won the war for the Allies—Stalingrad, El Alamein, Midway and Britain—almost half the productions were super-duper musicals. *Yankee Doodle Dandy* with James Cagney and *This Is the Army* with seventeen Irving Berlin songs were the big successes of the year.

There were attempts to inform the movie-going audience; *The Fighting Lady* (1944) and *The Battle of San Pietro* (1944) were impressive documentaries. The first, filmed by the famed photographer Edward Steichen, featured the actions of an aircraft carrier in the Pacific battles, while the second, made by John Huston, focused on a battle in Italy. Huston's emphasis on the tragedy of repeated assaults and defeats angered the Pentagon, which released a shortened version of the film. Documentaries were never too successful during the war, and the unbroken repetition of fighting sequences without any adequate commentary often bored and confused audiences. The most effective, and a truly superb documentary, was made by Frank Capra for the Department of the Army—the *Why We Fight* series. These films used a variety of devices—old newsreel footage from Germany, captured wartime film, animated maps and foreign films. The series about the war in Russia included long sequences from Eisenstein's *Alexander Nevsky* to impress upon viewers the violence of the Russo–German war. The Capra films, however, were for a limited audience and were not released to the public at large. For most, the Second World War remained an elaborate Western complete with different costumes and big explosions.

British film-makers realized the importance of fusing documentary and fictional devices; *Target for Tonight* and *One of Our Aircraft Is Missing* joined details of large-scale air raids and the story of one airplane crew. In both films professional actors and nonprofessionals were used. The second film dealt with the escape of five airmen from occupied Holland. Although both films did not discuss the political nature of the war, there was an emphasis on the planning and details of modern warfare.

Other film-makers did try to impress upon the public the difference between the two world wars. *The Life and Death of Colonel Blimp* was made in 1943 and focused on the mentality of the Victorian officer class which still thought of war as a gentlemanly profession. The film's major element was Blimp's friendship with a courtly Prussian officer, a friendship dating from the late 1890s. By depicting the Prussian as an antifascist, the film tried to indicate the barbarism of the Nazis.

Some people will say that political films cannot be made during wartime, that doubts cannot be permitted to exist, let alone fostered. The Germans followed this logic and produced two full-length documentaries, *Baptism of Fire* about the Polish campaign and *Victory in the West* about the fall of France. The emphasis on battle footage with only the most rudimentary narration eventually bored audiences and actually created an attitude of suspicion on the part of the civilian viewers.

In the early forties American film-makers ignored the war as much as possible; in a 1943 feature one of the highlights was Ginger Rogers dancing on the deck of a battleship. After 1945 Hollywood started producing large numbers of war films. Some of these movies are technical masterpieces; the veterans who returned to Hollywood added a knowledge of detail that makes *Sands of Iwo Jima, Battleground* and *Command Decision* impressive works. Unfortunately, technical skill did not improve understanding of the war. *Rommel* utilized James Mason's talents to create a good-guy image of the German military, an image fostered, in part, by the situation in Eastern Europe where Stalin seemed more of a threat than the German Officer Corps.

Hollywood is not the only source of historical debasement; even well-intentioned Europeans who should know better propagate myths and prolong stereotypes. About three years ago liberal and leftist film-goers flocked to see *To Die in Madrid*. This French documentary about the Spanish Civil War was an emotional delight; the "Internationale" was heard repeatedly on the sound track, and the International Brigades got a lot of footage. The film, however, was a historical failure. One impressive battle scene was lifted from *All Quiet on the Western Front*; there were only vague references to the fatal disputes between Trotskyists and Stalinists; and the editing tended to confuse contemporary style with old newsreel footage. Perhaps if historians could become film-makers, there would not be such a disastrous gap between truth and pleasure in historical films.

Of course, pleasure is the main concern of Hollywood; truth is left to find its supporters and promoters among the forgotten compilers of mortality statistics and the authors of obscure doctoral dissertations. There is nothing wrong when films about sea monsters and vampires are made for adolescent consumption, but when the same mentality permeates a film about Vietnam and gets help from the Pentagon, it is disastrous. When the government lends equipment and installations to John Wayne, it countenances the worst kind of debasement.

Hollywood also debases people by the use of hollow stereotypes and worthless characterizations. For years the only Englishmen shown on a 35-mm screen were stage gentlemen like C. Aubrey Smith, while Stepin Fetchit served as the movie-makers' Negro. The Marx Brothers comedies from the thirties all featured a "little darky" number; the elaborate one in *Day at the Races* is only the most famous and undisguised. In *Dr. No*, the first 007 thriller, there is a black Jamaican who works for the CIA. He is portrayed as such a lackey that it is as embarrassing as it is shocking to watch him. While Bond and his U.S. counterpart discuss the disappearance of an agent, they make no effort to include their black helper in the conversation. When Bond passes a cigarette case to the CIA man, the Jamaican is not offered one. Later Bond even has his shoes carried by his black lackey. Most films about Negroes abstract the problem of racism from any real setting; Sidney Poitier is a black teacher in an English slum in one film and an important physician from a wealthy family in another. Hollywood still cannot film the dilemma of the ghetto—unemployment and exploitation.

Stereotypes mean less work for the screenwriter and director, since they do not have to worry about characterizations. Even Mike Nichols' *The Graduate* falls victim to this flaw. Nichols, in his effort to depict the grotesque alienation of his hero, forgot an essential element in any film about a young man in America—the draft. A film about a young person's hassles with the Army is as unthinkable to Hollywood as the problem of housing in the ghetto.

Problems like these two require a familiarity with

actual conditions and the ability to film them. For instance, Jacques Démy did not know that most twenty-six-year-olds are not drafted when he wrote *The Model Shop*. *Raisin in the Sun* focused on discrimination in housing, not on the more important economic struggle to be able to move out of a slum.

Luckily for those whose interest in cinema is as a political weapon, the big studios are being forced to change by both their own need for profits and independent film-makers who have money and experience. Shirley Clarke's *Cool World*, *Connection* and *Jason* are views of worlds most people will never know—the cultures of slum Negroes, junkies and hustlers—but which exist as proof of a society's decay. To compete with this type of film Mike Nichols is given immense sums of money and freedom to make *The Graduate*, and now *Catch-22*. Paul Newman, Barbra Streisand and Sidney Poitier have formed their own company, while 20th Century Fox grinds out advertisements for Omar Sharif as Che Guevara. Obviously, the super-duper musicals and sentimental films about the poor are no longer viable, no longer profitable. Part of the reason for this change is the work of people like Cassavetes and Clarke, the need of the audience to understand the problems they face and Hollywood's impulse to cash in on the revolution they are helping to prepare. As a result of this variety of causes, there is a tension between film and revolution. Sometimes it produces a superb piece of work like *The Battle of Algiers*. It can also mean a travesty like *Greetings*. This combination of exploitation and Victorian hypocrisy (*Greetings* features a half dozen naked chicks whom the three heroes can screw, but only one girl to love, and she is never seen naked) is being sold as a protest film.

It is up to radicals in all fields to realize that films are as important as the books, magazines and newspapers the movies often supplant. People like Nichols and Newman must be criticized in all kinds of publications from *The New York Review of Books* to SDS *New Left Notes*. The omission of the draft from *The Graduate* concerns activists as well as film critics, Marxists as well as sociologists. I think it is time for historians to make documentaries about modern history. A good film about China from 1937 to 1949 would be more damaging to United States foreign policy than any rally. Most historians would not dispute the need for such a documentary, and many compare the present American position in Southeast Asia with that of Japan some thirty years ago. Some radicals have become filmmakers through Newsreel, a SDS documentary film group. Newsreel tries to make short documentaries that will politically arouse and educate their viewers (the thirties phrase is *agitprop*). Sometimes they succeed admirably, as in *Garbage*, a short about the Up Against the Wall Motherfuckers group on New York's Lower East Side, but some of their productions seem deliberately difficult to follow, especially their film about the Pentagon demonstration in October, 1967.

Many of us who are serious about changing America have to learn film techniques and make movies. Nichols, Clarke, Cassavetes and the Maysles brothers (*Salesman*) cannot be trusted to produce the type of films a revolution needs. Their work should be critically reviewed and studied, both as commentary and as a guide to independent action. Mike Nichols and John Cassavetes must be gauged by what Shirley Clarke and the Maysles are producing; Clarke and the Maysles by what Newsreel and the collective cinema groups are doing; and they, in turn, by what others with even less money and equipment are planning. Radicals must film social problems in the most shocking and undisguised reality. Columbia Pictures and 20th Century Fox can deal with nudity, drugs and even the Che Guevara myth—it is the social backgrounds to these things with which they cannot deal. The big studios may realize the importance of directors and screenwriters who now demand high salaries and immense latitude in their work, but the radical film-makers don't have to charge a $3 admission. If the scholarly opponents of a war like that in Vietnam would make a documentary about Asia, Jean-Luc Godard might film the life of Leon Trotsky—then where will Richard Nixon be?

Arnold Steinberg

At twenty-two, Arnold Steinberg became editor of *The New Guard,* the monthly magazine of Young Americans for Freedom, and he held that position for nearly two years. A native of Los Angeles, he worked actively for Goldwater in 1964 and Reagan in 1966. After attending UCLA where he was California YAF Executive Director, he received his B.A. from George Washington University. "I headed my high school debate team and in college used my debating experience to challenge leading young leftists. I consider myself a libertarian-conservative and firmly believe in laissez-faire capitalism."

✠✠✠✠✠✠✠✠✠✠✠✠✠✠✠✠✠✠✠✠✠✠✠✠✠✠✠✠✠✠✠✠✠✠✠✠✠✠✠

Dear Mr. President:

What is the nature of American society against which many students, often under the banners of the New Left, are rebelling? I suggest that in rebelling against the Establishment, the New Left adherents have not correctly identified the Establishment, which is liberal. Implicitly or explicitly, the liberal approach posits that the state can solve the problems of society through government paternalism, and that a collectivist approach to the goals of society is best. An egalitarian impulse prevails, centralization and bureaucracy abound. Because tradition and continuity are given scant attention, a relativistic approach is encouraged, and often the attempted transmission of values from one generation to the next is written off as an unwanted promulgation of value judgments. That these are generalizations about liberal traits should not obscure the fact that these traits are pervasive within the liberal approach. Freedom, which receives such high priority from the libertarian-conservative, is usually interpreted by liberals in the narrow sense of civil liberty. "Freedom from" anything the liberal finds objectionable is the replacement for the more traditional objective—freedom from state coercion.

My point is that to the extent the New Left proposes anything at all, it proposes programs that, in the end, will increase the power of the state and decrease individual freedom. "Participitory democracy" is a nice slogan, but for potential tyrannists, it can become the rationale, the zeitgeist, for corrupt and coercive state action. This essay concerns itself with what I consider to be the real ideological revolutionaries: the young libertarian-conservatives, in which category I include myself and most members of Young Americans for Freedom.

Disdaining violence and wholesale replacement of American institutions, we define a position of maximum individual freedom that is inconsistent with that of Herbert Marcuse, Tom Hayden and other New Left spokesmen. Our emphasis on the *individual* is also too radical for an Eisenhower or a Johnson, a Humphrey or most liberals. Presidents and Presidential candidates are very much of the Establishment, and it is our basic differences with government leaders and their colleagues in the academy and the news media that reflect our revolutionary thrust.

Libertarians are products of the conservative movement, and we realize that radical change cannot come quickly. Sudden change, even if it is in the right direction, can lead to massive disruption of society and create problems worse than those that inhere in the status quo. Change may not always be initiated by the President or the public sector, but with our government's vast power, change in the direction of more freedom for the individual cannot come without the blessing of the state.

Collective solutions and egalitarianism underlie not only the welfare state, but also society's activities in other areas. Considering the area most closely related to young people—education—we find a system designed to educate "everybody" and multiuniversities that seem to do everything but teach. Education at the lower levels, like society itself, emphasizes "life adjustment" and conformity.

Even complex problems, rooted in many causes, are ascribed to collective guilt—our "racist" society. It is easy to label a society "racist," but I believe such terminology inflames emotions on both sides, doesn't contribute toward solving any problems and actually misrepresents the real nature of American society. If blacks are given license to assume that all of their problems are products of a racist society, they may adopt violence to strike back at racism rather than look toward the solution of their problems. Well-meaning whites who can be enlisted in cooperative efforts are alienated by the "racist" terminology. Attitudes are slowly formed and slowly changed. We should try to deal with the racial hang-ups of people, not give them new hang-ups.

A corollary problem is describing as racist those individuals or institutions that are simply inept. For example, I would attribute the lack of proper emphasis on contributions of black people to American history not as racist-motivated, but rather as the result of ignorance. I might add that black people are not the only minority to be slighted in American history, and the contribution of minority groups is not the only area of American history that needs scrutiny and revision.

My own feeling is that many originators of the "racist society" thesis—the members of the Kerner Commission, for example—are the very engineers who guided society to its present instability. The liberal approach has clearly misread the problems, and it has prescribed the wrong answers. The most dramatic evidence of this is the current black emphasis on independence and the repudiation of integration as a cure-all. Many liberals, admittedly highly motivated, have *failed*. And rather than confess their failure, they have found a scapegoat—the racist society.

The whole area of race relations offers an occasion for the President not only to act consonant with a free society, but also to communicate with the people. "Ghettos" are in sad shape because of state action, *not* because of the market economy. Property taxes in many cities discourage slum improvements, and antiquated and/or burdensome housing codes stifle innovations. Black entrepreneurs who are qualified in every way are thwarted by government paperwork and regulations. Labor unions, protected by the government from competition, discriminate against qualified blacks. This practice of discrimination has been notoriously prevalent in the construction trades, where union membership has been required for employment.

Food prices are high for everyone, to be sure, but necessities (including food) comprise most of the budget of the poor family. We could remove part of the reason for high food prices by doing away (gradually) with farm subsidies and price supports. Not only would the market work toward lower food prices, but gradual removal of such subsidies would primarily affect the larger, *better-off* farmers who receive most of these subsidies.

Minimum wage legislation has been repeatedly passed with the noble objective of raising the wages of the unskilled laborer. Yale Brozen, an economist who has studied this subject for years, has concluded that minimum wage legislation has caused significant unemployment. When government tells employers they must pay a certain wage, many employers fire workers whose productivity is less than the legally set minimum wage. Brozen has shown in detail how blacks and teenagers are the hardest hit by minimum wage legislation. In many cases the effects are more than simply putting someone on the unemployment rolls. Productivity is lost, welfare payments rise, an individual's pride and initiative are adversely affected, and the individual may lose training and experience that could lead to a better job.

These examples are neither isolated nor exhaustive; they simply point up the problems caused by *state intervention*. It is easy to understand the reluctance of those who have lobbied for state intervention to accept the thesis that many of our problems are actually caused or aggravated by state intervention. But I believe this thesis is supported by the evidence, and the conclusion is that planned reduction of state intervention is desirable.

The President is in a unique position to reorient government fiscal and monetary policies away from discretionary authority to more minimal and precise government action. An example is Milton Friedman's advocacy that the money supply be increased by a fixed amount annually to allow for more dollars to meet increased productivity, and to do away with the Federal Reserve's discretionary power, which Friedman blames in large part for economic fluctuations in the economy. Government legislation must be revised or repealed, and executive policies that are harmful must be reevaluated.

The President can set the pace in encouraging states,

counties, cities and all levels of government to reexamine their taxing structures and other regulations. One of many examples I could cite is found in the medical field. Here state licensure of physicians has contributed to the inadequate supply of doctors. The medical associations and the state licensure laws together have resulted in a virtual monopoly for the medical profession. Like many government-supported monopolies, the medical monopoly is justified on the basis of the public good, in this case, public health. Such licensing, it is alleged, protects the public against quacks. The contention that such licensing really prevents quacks from practicing is questionable, but apart from that, licensing is much too broad a concept. Milton Friedman in his book *Capitalism and Freedom* suggests a certification procedure to allow for degrees of competence to perform various medical chores. Certainly we should proceed with great care in this area in an effort to preserve high standards, but the need for some differentiation of skills and duties is partially sustained by the increased number of medical schools offering courses of instruction leading to a profession as a "doctor's aide."

Federal regulatory commissions, originating ostensibly to protect the public interest, perpetuate existing monopolies and/or encourage the development of new monopolies. This is true, for example, of the Interstate Commerce Commission, which protects various transportation means (e.g., railroad) from competition with other transportation alternatives (e.g., trucking). The ICC, like the Civil Aeronautics Board, sets prices (rates) that are higher than the rates that would prevail if the free market were allowed to operate. Government can never claim to oppose monopoly when its own policies and its own agencies foster it.

Is a free society a humane society? First, we must

realize that the free market is only part of a free society, in that the free market assures economic abundance. If we give it a chance to operate, and do away with state intervention, which often hurts those we allegedly want to help, I believe we will ameliorate problems like poverty at a faster rate than we have in the past. This nation has already made remarkable progress in raising living standards, and a truly free market can introduce a new era of solving social problems.

For too long we have been avoiding problems. Many individuals have been hypocritical, telling others to desegregate while practicing segregation themselves. Others have urged artificial solutions (such as busing of school children to achieve integration) to placate those clamoring for real progress. Others have broken unrealistic promises made to minorities and to the poor.

To recognize the failures of the past will make more likely intelligent action in the future. Only recently have Americans in leadership positions realized the potential of the private sector to solve social problems. It is the free market system alone that directly imposes costs on the person who discriminates. If an employer hires an incompetent white person rather than a competent black, he bears the cost of the white person's incompetence. It is more difficult for such an employer to compete with one who hires on the basis of competence, and thus has lower costs.

Richard Cornuelle has used the term "independent sector" to describe the vast array of churches, private groups, foundations and civic organizations that have voluntarily allocated tremendous amounts of resources toward solving problems. Through his leadership and inspiration, the President can encourage free men to voluntarily solve their problems. This may sound visionary, but the record of free men and voluntary action is a good one. The record of government is a dismal one.

As long as government has preempted a great deal of problem solving by confiscatory taxation, the only way to spur certain actions is by tax incentives and tax credits. The government can make profitable investment in the ghetto or in job retraining. Through reductions in their income tax, the government can even make it feasible for some talented individuals to teach in inner-city schools. The list of objectives and methods is nearly endless, and the use of tax incentives may prove to be the best method for simultaneously reducing the public sector and solving social problems.

I have touched on many topics to illustrate the utilitarianism of freedom. But is freedom a goal itself? The answer is, first, that freedom is a positive value and that with economic freedom comes political and social freedom. Secondly, it's true that the free man may choose what some consider to be the wrong course. But *he* should have that choice. Finally, the free man may choose the immoral over the moral or virtuous. But morality has little meaning if we must coerce individuals to pursue a moral course.

The collectivist approach has, in my judgment, contributed to a sense of alienation among the young, who are individually losing their identity. The myth that a free society is unstable must be corrected, for only a free society and a state restricted to limited powers can provide for individuals an environment conducive to assurance and confidence, and at the same time provide the equilibrium our society so desperately needs.

David Steinberg

Twenty-six-year-old David Steinberg grew up in New York, went to school in Ohio, lived in Washington, D.C., and then moved to San Francisco where he lives in a communal family of five people, including his wife Susan, between the ages of twenty-four and twenty-six. They "share a six-room flat, income, work, a strong feeling of mutual commitments, a lot of hassles and joys. We're working to build new and more satisfying patterns for our lives, patterns involving our conception of money, work, marriage, sexuality, how we see ourselves, how we relate to each other and to outside people. Since September (1969) we have been running a free school for junior high school kids called The Learning Place. . . ."

Let's face it, America is falling apart at the seams. Prosperity, computers, the poverty program and Neil Armstrong aside, it's becoming harder and harder to maintain the happy illusion that the society is functioning smoothly. Look at the signs: Every big city worth its salt has a stockpile of weapons ranging from mace to high-powered rifles, tanks and armed helicopters; mild-mannered housewives are learning to carry pistols in their purses as a matter of course; college administrators attend expensive conferences to find out how to keep their universities functioning through the academic year; literally millions of parents are discovering that they have completely lost touch with their kids; corporations are unable to keep the best of their young talent from dropping out of corporate life after two or three years; sons and daughters of distinguished Americans get arrested for smoking grass or dropping acid. Divorces are up, as are prices, commuting times, psychoanalysis rates, blood pressures, cigarette smoking, runaways, gun purchases and a whole generation of young people. No two ways about it, the country is down.

So what's wrong? Looking at the problems one at a time, we've been able to comfort ourselves with easy explanations. But individual problems—poverty, racism, violence, the cities, the alienation of youth—are only symptoms of a deeper disease. Looking at them all together, we can begin to see that the sickness lies way down at the core of what we call the American way of life. So let's start at the beginning.

At the foundation of "the American way" sits John Calvin with his peculiar perspective on man and the universe. Humanity is divided into two groups, the good guys and the bad guys, the chosen and the damned. The good guys work hard, deny themselves pleasure and are rewarded with lots of money. The bad guys are slothful, hedonistic and consequently stricken with poverty. This moralistic philosophy, strong in the minds of the colonizers before they ever boarded the *Mayflower,* became established as the One True Right Doctrine when reinforced by the stark realities of pioneer life in a strange and hostile wilderness. For the early settlers, self-denial and hard work were in fact necessary for survival and the ability to survive was the measure of the man. The culture of frontier Calvinism defined a good man as a Christian, white, temperate hard worker endowed with wealth. As the appropriate ethics were taught to each new generation, they became woven into cultural mores that would live on long after the realities of daily life had changed. Ethnocentrism, sexual repression, materialism and defining one's existence through hard work became part of the American tradition.

As pioneer hardship gave way to the industrial era, the culture evolved new forms to keep pace with the changing times. Industrialization brought new wealth and new social heroes—the robber barons. Material expansion and prosperity confirmed America as God's chosen nation, adding moral sanction to an exploitive sense of national purpose. Westward expansion, with its genocidal extermination of native Americans, became a glorious national fulfillment through "manifest destiny."

With the explosive expansion of mass technology after World War II, a gradual process of cultural evolution turned into a cataclysmic cultural upheaval. Postwar America was a brand-new game, and the rules were the rules of technoculture. With goodness and success measured by material output, mass production took on the flavor of a religious crusade. Under technoculture, the goal is to get the most out of the least; the fundamental value is efficiency. Reverence of quantity eclipses earlier respect for quality; maximal use of material resources takes the place of concern for human fulfillment. It's the same old values transposed onto the numbers game. In pursuit of efficiency and capital gain, the culture of mass technology places new emphasis on conformity, rational calculation and material values, rejecting ever more strongly emotionality, eccentricity and sentimentality. Thus ticky-tacky houses, all the same but for the color of their pastel walls. Thus rectangular office buildings with row after row of identical windows. Thus the growth of rational, efficient and dehumanizing bureaucracy. Thus the collection of small concerns into giant corporations.

Men become quantified, rationalized and reduced to common entities, "all the better to efficiently process you, my dear." Individual identity, lost in the shuffle, adds new frenzy to the remaining outlet of competition. Men define themselves in contrast to each other, and their worth by whom they are better than. In the context of money culture, better than means richer than, and success means being richer than poor people, or at least (a flashback to early Calvin) not being black. Material rewards are glorified, while in a culture that supresses emotion, the very real human costs are ignored. From the culture of technology comes the loss of individual identity and meaning. From the growth of giant institutions come deep feelings of impotence, insignificance and loss of purpose. From the culture of dispassionate reason come emotional withdrawal, boredom and cynicism. From the culture of competition come fear of others, alienation, emotional distance, loneliness, aggressiveness and violence.

Significantly, there isn't much new in all these postwar developments. Modern America is not moving away from traditional American values, only refining and extending them into the realities of contemporary life. Once we associated wealth with goodness and relegated emotional fulfillment to the realm of the devil, all the rest followed with the march of time.

The upheaval we are now facing is the collision between these modern expressions of traditional American culture and the abundant wealth of our postwar world. An entire bulging social stratum in America lives in abundant affluence. For them, the accumulation of material resources has become obsolete, and with it the culture of scarcity. Among the older generation, the culture lives on by inertia, but for the youth the culture is dead.

First comes the realization by the children of the middle class that money and material goods are independent of both personal worth and personal fulfillment. Their experience with family and friends states quite clearly that those who have made it by traditional standards of American culture haven't made it at all. If anything, becoming "successful" has only brought more hang-ups, heartaches and sleepless nights than the days of poverty. It immediately follows that the work ethic is obsolete. Having sufficient material goods for a decent life no longer requires continual labor and self-denial. "Working for a living" no longer brings a sense of personal achievement. Material wealth, stripped of its moral connotation and its ability to give a personal sense of fulfillment, becomes neutral at best, destructive at worst. Having enough bread to live on is one thing; respecting work in itself is something else. The moral notion of hard work no longer makes sense. Middle-class youth know it, and so do the poor and the blacks.

For the children of postscarcity America, then, the central questions are no longer material, but psychic and emotional. Questions of leisure and emotional fulfillment. Questions of relationships with other people and with oneself. Questions of the quality of one's life and one's work. Questions of social purpose and personal meaning. A whole new spectrum of needs faces America, having nothing to do with money, material possessions or economic production. But the culture, built on four hundred years of bare survival and the pursuit of material abundance, stands directly in the way. It is time to build a new culture, one that supports rather than denies the needs of individuals. A most, most difficult undertaking, perhaps impossible, but unavoidable. The process has already begun.

Look at what's happening, particularly among young people, from the perspective of a significant process of culture building. What we are used to calling the "youth problem" is in fact an attempt to transcend the restrictions and frustrations of American life by building an alternative social and cultural context more appropriate to the times. From scattered groups of isolated individuals an integrated fabric of values and norms is coming, a relatively stable social code with expectations radically different from those of American society.

The new culture revolves strongly around associative forms of identity, defining who you are in cooperative rather than competitive terms, as part of close groups, in intimate contact with others. The emphasis is on what one has in common with others rather than on how one is different. Group membership becomes a supportive base for being able to be oneself, instead of the antithesis of individuality. The concept of the universal brotherhood of man falls into harmony with the fullest development of individual personality. What a contrast to America's schizophrenic vacillation between conformity and individual assertion.

Money, so central to all aspects of American life, is reduced in the new culture to a necessity for existence, and with the discovery that full, rich lives are possible on surprisingly little money, to a rather incidental consideration. Freed from respect for material possessions as a sign of human worth, the new culture is able to see people more in terms of who they are than what they have. Consequently, the notion of "better than" can be replaced by respect for all individuals as equally valid and valuable. Separated from the problem of bringing in cash, work can be principally a creative outlet, to be evaluated in terms of interest and personal fulfillment, with proper emphasis on "doing your own thing."

Personal interactions flower at all levels in the new culture as relations among equally important individuals. The master-slave bag, based on possessive, hierarchical and competitive forms, and so damaging to real and rewarding personal contact, is rejected in all its forms: dominance of men over women, of parents over children, of teachers over students, of whites over blacks, of employers over employees. People in different roles are respected equally; all the rest follows.

Naturalism, rejection of artifice, respect for intuition and emotion, openness to sensuality and sexuality, a sense of being in tune with your mind, body and environment, all are integral to the new culture. It's the brotherhood of men extended to the universality and essential oneness of all things, directly contrary to the puritan self-denial of Calvinist America, with its strict separation of man from nature. A spirit of communion, intimacy with large numbers of individuals, trust, openness to emotional contact, mutual sensitivity and concern also help to make possible a sense of wholeness, personal fulfillment and worth scarcely conceivable in the context of present American values and culture. Human needs, values and concerns are in ascendance; material ones are in decline. Efficiency and material productivity will suffer. But our most pressing needs now are the human ones, and the personal rewards and possibilities of the new forms are immense.

The culture is attractive, of course, to a generation that has witnessed the pyrrhic victory of mass affluence. It is a natural expression of this generation's needs, needs that seem certain to become more acute as long as the hegemony of technological values runs mainstream America. Small wonder that from being a scattered fringe only three years ago the new culture has mushroomed to become a major national "problem." The new forms prove by their example that the preachings of the "realists" ("this is the only way it can be done") are nothing but empty myths. With the myths removed, young people by the millions are choosing the forms that seem to have the most promise for a good life. How could they do otherwise? There is no turning back.

What is saddest is that America seems to be unable to deal with the new cultural forms except to react in fear by trying to suppress them. The new culture can perhaps be driven underground, but as an expression of a new age, it can hardly be extinguished, and suppression will only drive the new forms further and further away from those parts of American life and tradition that could usefully be preserved. Worse yet, reaction against repression may well cause the new culture to become as ugly and distorted from people's real needs as the one it seeks to replace. What then, America? A self-fulfilling prophecy—the young builders turned into directionless rebels, leaving only a choice between two forms of living death? No, new forms need to be cherished and nourished, new institutions encouraged and built. We live in a new world. Its direction is ours to shape.

Paul Steiner and Meredith Maran

Both in their late teens, Paul Steiner and Meredith Maran are veterans of the high school revolution in New York City, where Mr. Steiner also founded and produced the first high school underground newspaper, *Sansculottes*. Now living in San Cristobal, New Mexico, Mr. Steiner and Miss Maran are the authors of the recently published *Off the Schools*.

❧❧❧❧❧❧❧❧❧❧❧❧❧❧❧❧❧❧❧❧❧❧❧❧❧❧❧❧❧❧❧

Most Beloved mister nix-on,

In the midst of your crumbling empire is a new force of polarity, as yet unknown to most of your subjects. They are purple in your mountains' majesty, independent despite your declarations, united within and without your states. In between flashes of your neon indifference, you and yours may shiver as you feel their screaming magnetism—writhe in anguish as the high-pitched velocity of their changes penetrates your aching eardrums.

As you sit enthroned, awaiting alternatives to be presented gently for your consideration, the castle is shaken by unearthly, violent vibrations . . . you are thrown to the floor and only then do you come face to face with what will kill you. As you creak out your final breath, you wonder: "Why . . . didn't . . . I . . . notice . . . it . . . before . . . ?"

DYING	NEWBORN
Wonder Bread	home-baked
TWA	VW
Phisohex	warpaint
Johnnie Walker Red	acapulco gold

Miltown	I Ching
Christmas vacation	every winter day
Summer vacation	every summer day
hatework	lovework
theater/monthly	life/always
makeup	sun
wig	wind
mass-produced armor	costumes
applause	clapping
cha-cha-cha	kick out the jams
teacher	friend
student	friend
education	learning
plans	now
lies	stories
mass media	truth
CBS	eyes
ABC	ears
NBC	fingers
mewsic	sound explosion
heh-heh	HA!
listening	hearing
gardening	creating
wife-swapping	freedom
be realistic	demand the impossible
shave	letitallhangout
gray	COLORS!
handshake	embrace
the Father	Dylan
the Son	the Stones
the Holy Ghost	Che
political parties	affinity groups
barriers	barricades
walls	communes
politics	life
whatashame	revolution

letter to N.Y. *Times* . . . . .revolution
lesser of two evils . . . . revolution
repression . . . . .revolution
war . . . . .revolution
DEATH . . . . .REVOLUTION!

And you send your most trusted emissaries to search us out. We hear the rumblings above our heads and come forth willingly. . . . They ask, "What is your program?" Straight-eyed and with laughter under our tongues, we answer, "We know we've got it if it makes us feel good."

Such things produce much confusion in your world; you see in your waking nightmares, "They must be destroyed, but how, when?"

So you pick of yours those most likely to survive the descent, and, posing as of ours, they join us. When they return to you, they have brought the lavish gifts of our words and deeds. To madison avenue they give our costumes . . . to suburbia, our acapulco gold . . . to your old age homes, our I Ching . . . but to your youth, they can only offer—our REVOLUTION!

Daniel E. Tijerina

Eighteen-year-old Mr. Tijerina writes "we have had it rough all of our lives and never had a home of our own. Ever since my father started this fight for justice here in New Mexico, it is very difficult for us to get a job. Our lives have been threatened. Our headquarters, where we also live now, has been bombed. The police and National Forest Service men have persecuted us and locked us up. I have also had to drop out of school twice because of my name. You see, the teachers don't like it very well. . . ."

This, Mr. President, is to tell you how I feel about the problems now facing the United States, particularly our struggle for justice in the Southwestern states. Here in the state of New Mexico we have an organization that is led by my father, Reis Lopez Tijerina. We are fighting for what we know is ours here in the Southwest, our land grants left to us by our Spanish and Indian ancestors. We, the Indo–Espano people, are followers and believers of what is right, and we have not been brainwashed or whitewashed in the schools of the United States. We have been trying to fight in the courts for these land grants which do belong to us, but the government doesn't even bother to look into the Treaty of Guadalupe, which was signed on February 2, 1848, by the United States and Mexico.

Mr. President, I ask not for me but for my people that you look into the Treaty of Guadalupe Hidalgo. I think it is only just that you do this because our people have been put down long enough. I assure you that if the legal papers of the Treaty of Guadalupe have not been changed or destroyed, you will find that these grants do legally belong to us. We are not a people of violence, but we do believe in justice. If this problem is not looked into, I assure you that the United States will become just like North and South Vietnam. We will fight for our rights until we have won or died. We are not like some of these others that are always rioting or demonstrating for better jobs, better pay and things like that. All we want is what belongs to us legally, the land left to us by our fore-fathers, which was protected by the Treaty of Guada-lupe.

The Anglos came and cheated and stole and killed for these land grants. Some homesteaded the land, some bought it for fifty cents an acre, and when our people didn't want to sell, they forced out their cattle and burned their crops. Sometimes they would kill the man of the house and force his woman to sell. And now that we have finally gotten started organizing to gain our rights here in New Mexico, the Minutemen and the John Birch Society are trying to stop us. I believe that these organizations have members who are policemen and rich people like bankers and big businessmen. That is why it is hard for us to progress rapidly.

I know Rome wasn't built in a day, and neither will we win our fight rapidly. But your helping us, Mr. President, will save a lot of lives. Our organization head-quarters has been bombed many times. My father has been assaulted many times, yet the police say they can never catch anybody. One time an ex-policeman was caught red-handed trying to bomb our headquarters. Instead, he blew his own arm off with the dynamite. The police chased him in a car, and when he was caught, they said that getting his arm blown off was enough punishment for this white person. Another time we were bombed during a meeting at our headquarters. The car of the vice-president of the organization was blown to shreds. The organization truck is now not in running condition because of that same bomb, and before that the inside was burned with gun powder. Many other cars have also been damaged badly.

On June 3, 1967, we were going to have a meeting in a small town known as Coyote, but a district attorney stopped everything with the aid of the state police. Leaflets were handed out to people who were going to attend the meeting, saying my father is a communist and that people attending the meeting would be arrested. Many people were arrested.

On June 5 we were invited to a picnic at a member's ranch in Canjilon. While at the picnic, a rumor went around that some of the men were going to make a citizen's arrest. They were going to arrest the district attorney who had stopped the meeting we were supposed to have had on the third day of June. The men who had been arrested a couple of days before were being arraigned. So a group of people got together there at the picnic and went to the court house in Tierra Amarilla to make a citizen's arrest. When a few of them walked into the court house, a state policeman went for his gun. When the men saw the policeman reach for his gun, they shot him. After they shot him, many others started shooting. Then they looked all over for the district attorney but they couldn't find him. So the men got into their cars and trucks and went back to the picnic at Canjilon.

Within a few hours the National Guard and state policemen came with their army tanks and helicopters. I guess they wanted to have a little war there. But like I say, we're not people of violence unless forced into it. We were surrounded by state policemen with carbines and shotguns. We were all told to step into a clearing

and sit on the ground where there was horse shit and
cow shit. Afterward they took the few rifles that we
had. Then we were all called out of the corrals. They
searched us and took our names, just like a captured
enemy in war. Then they sent us all back into the corrals. We had been cooking potatoes when they got
there. It started raining and they didn't let us tend
our food.

We were held at the corral for two days and a night
and the National Guard wouldn't let us accept blankets
from people who were offering them to us. We had to
ask for permission to use the bathroom. But afterward,
my father was freed because, Mr. President, ours is a
just cause.

Mr. President, it is only right that you look into our
problem. It is not right that our people go on being
treated this way. Our people need to learn the truth in
schools. The Treaty of Guadalupe Hidalgo says that
teachers in the state of New Mexico have to know both
English and Spanish culture and language. But the majority do not. We need to be taught our Spanish culture in our schools. The schools teach about Davy
Crocket and Lewis and Clark, but they don't teach
about our Spanish heroes, like Mario Leyba, who you
probably never even heard of.

Well, Mr. President, just like our country needs us,
we need our country. We need justice here in the
United States, not in Vietnam. At the age of eighteen
we have to go to Vietnam to die like animals or go to
jail if we won't. But at the age of eighteen we can't
even vote for anything. Why is it, Mr. President, that
we can die at eighteen but we can't vote? Those are
the kinds of things you should worry about first before
sending us to any war.

God made people to help each other, not fight

against each other. If all the countries can't unite in peace, why don't you try to get peace here by satisfying your own people, not Koreans or Vietnamese.

But the one thing I ask of you most, Mr. President, is to look into our problem of land grants. After we get our rights I would be more than glad to fight in a just war for the United States.

I only wish I could say all this in person to you, Mr. President. I could have said it much better. But still this is better than nothing. Please do try to look into our problems. We are tired of not being able to live right. I hope you will see that we can talk Spanish freely in our schools. Now we can't even do that because Spanish is considered a foreign language here. Tell me why, if Spanish was here before English?

You could help if you wanted to. The Anglos know how much they stole from us. Now that we are smarter, they are trying to shut us up by scaring us. Well, Mr. President, I tell you nobody will stop us. The time has come when the truth must come out and justice will be done, whether by you or by somebody else. But we will struggle until we have succeeded.

R. Emmett Tyrell

Born in 1944 in Dublin, Ireland, Mr. Tyrell moved to
the United States shortly thereafter, where he attended
Fenwick High School in Oak Park, Illinois, and received his B.A. in 1965 from Indiana University. In
September, 1967, he founded *The Alternative* and
worked throughout the year as executive director of
Indiana Young Americans for Freedom. In September,
1968, he returned to the Indiana history department
to work toward his Ph.D. He now lives in Blooming-
ton, Indiana, with his wife and child Zebylon, editing
The Alternative, studying and working with the Intercollegiate Studies Institute and the Young Americans
for Freedom.

It seems to me snortingly presumptuous for a twenty-
four-year-old to send off to all the world *his* manifesto.
Such an endeavor makes me wince, for presumptuous
people generally appear silly. Further, there are strategic questions: to whom is my manifesto heading, and
if it is whoosing toward anyone who matters, why in
God's name would he read it? Has he not read similar
decrees before? Is he unfamiliar with the youthful pon-
tifications from the twenties, the thirties and the fifties?
People who matter must know more than to listen to
the twaddle of callow youth.

Yet such views do not command a very high price
these days. To demur from assuming the spirit of manifesto is to appear uncommercial, and to be uncommercial today is to hazard irrelevance. In our age of
Aquarius one must be relevant, one must conform, one
simply must adjust. Well, I shall adjust, but allow me
a sop to the vanishing age of individuality. Allow me to

turn down the modulation from that of manifesto to
that of discourse and to map as best I can that shifting
terrain of contemporary American whim that inspires
unease in me.

America's inverted appraisal of youth continues to
mystify me. To me the young creature is an awkward
and rather pitiable thing. Youth is a time of unfulfilled
yearnings and perilous vulnerability. It is the time
when a young boy with a bat is more a danger to himself than to the outfield. A young man is not a graceful
creature; seen by discerning persons he is an embarrassment. His achievements come in Little Leagues that
are, alas, surrogates.

Yet herein lies another problem, for American adults
generally accord their young's vicarious worlds of Little
League, student journalism, student politics and the
like so very much celebrity that for the young it is
almost like being there, almost like a place in the
Majors, a Pulitzer or a chair in the Senate. Is it any
wonder that the student politician, say Mark Rudd
fresh from making Columbia safe for democracy, fails
to appreciate the difficulties of achieving international
harmony? Exposed to television documentaries neatly
encapsulating every crisis under the sun, they naturally
become impatient when President Nixon fails to per-
ceive world problems as simply as NBC does. Youth
brings nothing more to questions of national polity
than the eagerness of a rookie; yet adult America continues to spray rapturous effusions on youth's splendor
and sweetness, ignoring its ungainliness and inexperience. Most ultimate physical prowess is not attained
until around thirty, and great intellectual works are
rarely created before middle age. So far as I can see,
youth's only allures, aside from its innocence, are its
gaiety—a gaiety that often returns in senility—and its
potential—a potential that is seldom realized.

An intelligent person encountering the political nostrums of a Rudd will surely adjudge that what he says is invalid, that his understanding of history is incomplete, that his solutions are unreal. A student activist is but a Little Leaguer; his chances of a place on Capitol Hill will depend on something more than Mother's goodwill—if he is not more a student and less an activist, his chances are slim.

Of course, youth is not the end but the beginning, and beginnings are generally shaded with uncertainty. But why is it that Americans exalt youth even to the point of taking its most unfledged representatives seriously? Is their obsession with youth perhaps the threshold of greater problems? I think so. And I think one of those problems is America's traditional inability to separate appearance from reality.

How else does one explain that while young people thump their noble chests, blindly denouncing an incomparable heritage of freedom and almost institutionalized compassion, *Time* and *Life* continue to editorialize on the liberal idealism of this rage. Intellectuals bask in editorial floodlights, getting up occasionally to trample on another's rights and rave of their own unendurable repression; still the cameras whirr, the flashbulbs crackle, the reporters beg their golden nuggets. No matter how hypocritical or empty the gospel of youth, it still makes headlines in *The New York Times*. And this publicity derives from Americans' traditional obsession with style to the exclusion of essence. Americans have always lavished attention on the unusual, the fantastic, the absurd—on Harriet husbanding Ozzie, on political necromancers, on fallen Hollywood angels, and now on messianic adolescents.

If an injustice is profound, a cause real, it would not be likely to attract America's attention; the media would remark on it only accidentally. Though it did not bother the American conscience in the fifties, Negro life was 40 percent more uncomfortable at that time than it is today. But in the fifties the national conscience sweated over the problems of juvenile delinquency. Today juvenile gangs are larger and their warfare more internecine; yet to attract the nation's concern gangs would have to resort to nuclear warfare. Today we editorialize about the "black- . . . ," not the Negro mechanic or college graduate but the man who intends to found a "Black Republic" in New Jersey or collect tithes from pusillanimous clerics. Though he is about as thoughtful as a woman wrestler, Americans are fascinated by his style; Americans even take him seriously.

Issues intellectual and eschatological have for most Americans a drone of tedium. America attunes itself to the crackpot and the rogue. History will probably judge the seriousness of our problems in inverse relation to the attention paid to them by contemporary Americans. Assuredly, the real problems of our time seldom pass the lips of Huntley and Brinkley, and the man who thinks about them is uncelebrated. The wildest effrontery and most illiterate canard provoke Americans to the deepest soul-searching, and what in days of yore would have passed as nineteenth-hole cocktail chatter is today the subject of editorials, sermons and graduate school seminars.

Intellectually and spiritually, we have loosed our moorings. Once de Tocqueville traversed America marveling at our mores; today he would wonder at our morons, and lament that our savants exhaust their lungs on trivialities. For after a century of bombardment from ritualistic liberals the family no longer transmits tradition. Schools are reluctant to, or proscribed from, doing so. Hip educators talk of *deprogramizing* the young from their heritage, and everyone expresses dismay when these young grow alienated. Intending that education should not bias young minds, the Supreme Court has interdicted public prayer, schools denature the formerly revered name of God and, stalking relevance, the churches streamline religion; nevertheless, everyone is stunned when the young resort to hallucinogens and occultism in search of a "religious experience." Finally the "intellectual community," a skid-row haven for ritualistic liberals and relativists, continues to spawn nihilists, hedonists and incivists. Families, educators, churches and intellectuals no longer transmit authority or tradition. Rather they are social problems intent on solving one another. The middle class (traditionally America's revolutionary class) has lost its nerve. Adult America has grown to fear its young. And meanwhile something slips away. In America the old confidence is waning, vitality ebbing, irrepressible humor subsiding. Even that peculiar American capacity for compassion—almost always inherent in our foreign policy and now reaching overripe fruition in our welfare state—has dissipated. Our masochists gloat over this metamorphosis, our soothsayers deprecate it, the naive rush about with panaceas. But for some the nostalgia rolls in.

While America tortures itself over ephemeral social problems whose solutions have historically resided in our amazing technological innovations, social mobility or shifting public attention, its leaders fail to safeguard the wellsprings of authority, that authority which has shielded our ancestors' most precious bequest— freedom. In failing to respond to the contemporary dissolution of authority, our leaders are allowing pollutants to threaten that exhilarating environment of freedom which nurtures American democracy, a democracy that has continued for two hundred years to expand freedoms and extend equal opportunity.

Embalmed with an obsession for utopia and loathing majority rule, penthouse revolutionaries have stumbled across the astounding revelation that the world's greatest democracy is yet imperfect. Seeking the perfection of a form of government they do not seem to understand, they have evolved a new species of man, referred to as the New Left (*Hyaena hyaena*). Taking up the Old Left's assault on authority, the New Left has acquired more advanced weaponry; to wit, violent revolution. And while they pound away at the crumbling bastions of authority, they neglect the reality that from the ruins of authority inevitably arises the rule of raw power—freedom's final pollutant.

Unfortunately, this is not the kind of pillow that will enhance the American Dream. The messianic adolescents, the yapping left, like to think the world for which they are whining and revolting will usher in the dawn of freedom's golden age rather than its destruction. Those tolerant of these pollutants think they are cultivating enlightenment and preserving freedom, but in reality they are rotting its insulation. Neither the young nor the old seem capable of sifting reality from appearance. To them a student who has commandeered a rostrum speaks from authority, when in reality he speaks merely from an exercise of arbitrary power. The reality that power will replace frazzled authority is ineluctable.

In the thirties—after a decade of spiritual, cultural and material debauchery, after more and more offensive assaults by the irresponsible left on traditional authority—disordered Germany sought deliverance in a man of vision, of charisma, of strength, of all those Promethean virtues we Americans hear about every four years. Germany got Hitler, Nazism and the rule of power. Our own South suffered a similar fate in the 1870s with the rule of the Bourbons.

Contemporary America is troubled by racial disorders, student unrest, inflation, moral decline and other apparent crises. But beneath all these problems is the far graver reality of decaying authority. As this reality brings America toward a period of civil disorder, we might bear in mind Aristotle's ancient observation that continued civil disorder (*stasis*) is the most terrible threat to democratic society, the precursor of despotism and the end of freedom.

Valentina Valdes

Valentina Valdes is twenty-one years old. One of six children, she was born in Denver, Colorado and raised in San Luis, Colorado. She attended San Luis Public School and Lincoln High School. This is what she herself has written about her life:

My father has been fighting for a land grant in southern Colorado, called the Sangre de Cristo grant, since 1958, before Reis Lopez Tijerina started fighting for our land and started the Alianza Federal de Mercedes. My father had given up, because of the selling out by lawyers and crooked judges. Then, when Reis Tijerina formed the Alianza, my father was very happy that one man was willing to fight full-time for our lands. So my father joined the Alianza.

I was just about eleven or twelve at the time my father started fighting for the land. He was always telling me and my brothers how the land had been stolen. I never believed him. I would say to myself, "How could such a thing as land stealing happen? Not here, not in the United States." The more he told us about the lawyers selling out and the crooked judges giving crooked decisions, the more I thought he was crazy.

I believed that way until 1964. I was in the eleventh grade then. A movie was shown on TV, saying that Chicanos ("Spanish Americans") were poor because they were lazy, ignorant and superstitious. That got me very mad because I knew that our people were not lazy. I knew that our people earned low salaries working in the fields and building roads to feed the United States economy.

At that time in school we were studying the Treaty of Guadalupe Hidalgo. All they told us was that this treaty gave Texas and New Mexico and other areas to the United States at the end of the

Mexican–American War in 1848. By that time I knew, from my father, that the Treaty of Guadalupe Hidalgo was supposed to protect our land and us, and that it had been violated. The teacher I had then asked us if we had seen that movie on Spanish Americans on TV. Only a few raised their hands. I then asked the teacher if I could give a report on the treaty and he said yes.

I started preparing myself and asking my father all kinds of questions. I did the report from what he said and from a series of articles written by Professor Clark Knowlton, which told how the treaty had been violated and that there were land grants in even big cities such as San Diego, California, and Albuquerque, New Mexico.

When I gave the report, I was scared and shaky because I thought the teacher was going to get mad and say it wasn't true. But I gave it anyway, and I said the movie was a lie—that our people were poor because our land had been taken away from us and not because we were lazy.

The teacher was so amazed that it showed on his face. He asked me, "Valentina, where did you get this material?" and said that in all the days of his teaching career he had never heard such a good report given in school. He asked me if I thought we were going to get our lands back, and I told him we sure were going to try.

After that I kept seeing in many different ways how right my father was.

When I graduated from high school, I spent a year trying to find a decent job, not finding one but finding out what discrimination was. I decided to stop looking for a job where all I would be doing would be putting a noose around my neck and our people's neck, and I decided to come to work where I would be helping our people. So I came to Albuquerque without knowing anybody here, to work in the Alianza Federal de Mercedes (now the Alianza Federal de los Pueblos Libres). I grew to love New Mexico and the people, and I stayed. I now see very clearly, from the crooked verdicts given by the courts to Reis Tijerina and other leaders in the United States, and many other things, how the laws are made just to protect the rich and not the poor. I now see very clearly how the time of the poor must come and I must help that. Since last spring I have been a worker in the new Tierra Amarilla Agricultural Cooperative, which has brought the people together to work their lands communally— as they once did—and to believe in their own power. That is my life now.

* * *

When I first went to school, I didn't know a word of English, but in the little Colorado village where I lived everybody was Chicano. So I had Chicano teachers all through grade school and learning English from them wasn't that hard for me. Up until the third grade we could speak Spanish freely. I had a third grade teacher who would have us go up in front of the class to tell stories, recite poems or sing songs. Most of the kids would speak in Spanish and she would even tell us some stories in Spanish. But after the third grade, if anyone was heard speaking Spanish on the school grounds, he was taken to the principal's office.

I know of a family that moved from a small village in New Mexico, where practically everybody including the teachers spoke Spanish, to a bigger city. When their little boy started school, he didn't speak a word of English and the teacher didn't know Spanish. The little boy used to tell his father that he could see the teacher's lips moving but didn't understand what she was saying. Because he could not understand or learn anything, he didn't want to go to school any more. The members of his family would try to walk him halfway to school, but when he was almost there he would turn around and go back home crying. Finally, the family sent one of its older girls to school with him, to translate what the teacher was saying. But that was no solution.

At the end of 1968 in Albuquerque, New Mexico, a survey was made of Chicanos starting school. One mother told how when her little boy started school, he didn't understand English. When he spoke in Spanish the teacher hit his hand and he grew to have an inferiority complex. It was hard for him to learn. When he didn't learn, he was put in a special class, and when he didn't learn there, he was sent to a school for the retarded. But he wasn't born retarded; they made him that way.

These stories show how society creates dropouts—who are really forced-outs. Besides not being taught in our own language, we don't learn anything about our culture or history. All we learn about in school is Dick, Sally and Jane, or Mr. White and Mrs. Jones, who have blond hair and blue eyes. And Kit Carson, Davy Crockett and Daniel Boone, the famous Indian murderers. We are taught that Joaquin Murietta, Pancho Villa and Emiliano Zapata were bandits, even though they were fighting with and for the poor against the rich, like Robin Hood, except that they were also fighting for the true liberation of our *raza* (race). Emiliano Zapata made the most beautiful and true statement: *"La tierra es de todos como el aire, el agua la luz y el calor del sol. Y tienen derecho a ella los que la trabajan con sus propias manos."* "The land is of everyone like the air, the water and the light and the heat of the sun. And those who work the land with their own hands have a right to it."

They don't teach us anything about the Laws of the Indies, which once prevailed in what is now the Southwest. They don't teach us about the Treaty of Guadalupe Hidalgo—which ended the so-called Mexican–American War in which the United States took all our land—and how it said that the United States must respect the land grants issued by Spain and Mexico, as well as the culture of the Spanish-speaking people living on these lands. They don't teach us about our Indian ancestry and culture, except to say that the Indians were "savages."

In school other kids who are whiter than you make fun of the color of your skin. This is what happened to me, until I began to hate my color and began to wish that I was whiter. So what happens when we are old enough to wear makeup? We put on tons and tons of white makeup. Then we're not satisfied with this, so we dye or bleach our beautiful black hair red or blond to look more Anglo. Even though we look worse after the makeup starts to crack and the black roots start to show, we think that we look beautiful because we look more Anglo. Why does all this come about? Because we don't learn anything about the beautiful culture our Indian ancestors left us.

Our fathers adopted a lot of that culture—many things, from the way people used to work communally down to *tortillas* (our bread). I remember that all the kids who took lunch to school, including me, would never take *tortillas* or *frijoles* (beans). It was shameful to take these things. If someone brought *tortillas* or *frijoles*, the other kids would whisper and make fun of him (even though they themselves ate these foods at home) until he would never want to take Mexican food for lunch again. In the lunch room they would never serve *tortillas, chile* or beans, even though the school was 99 percent Chicano. But now that the businessmen have found out that they can make money out of this delicious Mexican food, there are Mexican food stands and *taco* houses all over the place.

All this is very effective for the Anglo government. Not letting us learn in our own language is very bad;

we get so used to being ashamed of speaking our language that even if we know how to speak it, or understand it, we don't want to use it. This usually happens in the big cities. It gets so bad that we are even ashamed to pronounce our last names as they should be pronounced, and our first names always get translated. You don't say your name like it should be said, but you pronounce it like an Anglo name. Joe for José, Galigoose for Gallegos.

This denial of culture, language and history is very bad for our people. But, worse, our everyday life is bad. Jobs are hard to find and our people are hungry; more than half of them in northern New Mexico earn an income below the official poverty level. All this goes back to the Treaty of Guadalupe Hidalgo.

After that treaty was signed, and in spite of all the promises in it, the people were cheated out of their land in every way from trickery to just plain armed robbery. For instance, some Texans would offer a crop of beans to the people (who didn't know English) for the small service of making an X on a paper. That paper would be a document for their land ownership, and so they lost it. People would lose their land for not paying the taxes demanded by the United States government—when they had never known land taxation before and all the new American laws were published only in English. There were so many kinds of robbery. In 1832 more than 580,000 acres of land in just one grant belonged to the heirs of Tierra Amarilla, New Mexico. By 1969 the heirs had only 10,000 acres left. In another grant, that of San Joaquin, the heirs held about 500,000 acres in 1806. Today they have only 1,411.

The communal lands were all eaten up by the National Forest. The forest service now charges people to graze their animals, cut wood, fish or hunt deer on the land they once used freely. They could take as many cows as needed to graze there; today many people kill or sell their animals because they cannot afford the fees. The lumber companies get almost all the wood and the people can't afford to build.

In rural villages like Tierra Amarilla, New Mexico, a Chicano graduating from high school finds there is nothing for him to do. The only jobs available are the jobs the rich Anglo rancher or the Anglo government give, like working on roads or dams. Then there are the Chicano teachers and cops, who are mostly *lambes* (boot-lickers); once they get into the world of money, they say "I made it, why can't you?" and they don't give a damn about the rest of their own people—they even ignore or snub them. They don't give a damn about their *raza* or culture. So most boys join the military and go to fight dirty wars, or they go to another state to find work. Girls leave for the city to work as waitresses or scrubwomen. Young married couples leave their homes and go to the city.

The people once had a very beautiful way of living. People used the common lands as they needed, with no fences and no friction among neighbors. Whenever a family needed wood to build a house, all the neighbors would go with the family to the *sierra* to get as much as they needed, without any authorities telling them anything. When they returned, the neighbors would then help the family build the house. If a family needed meat, the men would go deer hunting or fishing and get what they needed without any trouble. When the hot weather came and it was too warm for the sheep to wear their winter coats, the people would sheer off the wool to make blankets, jackets and socks for the winter.

People were not stingy either. When they killed a cow, a pig or a sheep, they would invite two or three neighbors to help do the butchering. After they finished, the neighbors would be sure to get a good share of the animal that was killed. This is the way they worked, and a family was always sure to have meat in the house. When relatives or friends came to visit, they were always received well and were welcome to stay as long as they wished; the longer they stayed, the happier everybody was.

When it was time to plant, about nine, ten or more families would get their workhorses together and would go help one neighbor to plow and plant many acres of land. Then they would go to another house, and another, until the whole village was planted. For the weeding and harvest they would work the same way; and with the crops of the harvest they would trade with nearby villages and among themselves for the different things grown (like beans, potatoes and wheat for peaches, chile and tomatoes).

But life has changed; people have gotten used to the American way of life. Still, the people here in Tierra Amarilla, as well as in other small villages, have held onto a lot of their culture and language. I was raised in a small village something like this and little kids learned to speak in Spanish. When I was about fourteen we moved to a big city, and there most Chicano kids didn't speak in Spanish—they didn't even understand it; the younger they were, the less they understood Spanish. After living in the city for two years, whenever I heard a little boy or girl speaking Spanish, I felt like crying and hugging them.

Yes, life is different now; when relatives or friends go to visit people and stay over a week or two, people begin to wonder when their visitors are going to leave. The food in the house is getting less and less and a job doesn't support so many people. When people kill an animal, instead of sharing it with their neighbors, like their ancestors did, they hide it so it will last longer for the family. If a family doesn't have any animals (and there are many who don't), then they just don't eat meat because meat is too expensive to buy from the store. The only way they can eat meat is if they go deer hunting, and if they hunt out of season, they may be in danger. If a Forest Ranger catches them, they could get ten years in jail. But it is all right if a Texan comes to get elk during the hunting season, even if he only takes the head for his trophy room and leaves the rest of the meat to rot.

All these things have made many of our people angry and ready to fight for their rights. In other parts of the United States, it is mostly the youths who are involved in the Movement. But in northern New Mexico the older people are the ones who know the culture and history and who have been most interested in *La Causa* (The Cause). These are the people who formed the Alianza Federal de los Pueblos Libres, of which Reis Lopez Tijerina is the leader. He has awakened many people inside the state as well as outside.

There are new youth organizations too, but they have many problems. One very strong young man in *La Causa* started a group here in northern New Mexico last year. Then he had to leave the state because he couldn't pay his bills and he couldn't find a job here. The enemy knows how to divide us and weaken us.

But people go on trying. An agricultural cooperative was started in Tierra Amarilla by some young people. The purpose of it is to bring back some of the good old ways of working together and also to inject some hope into our oppressed people. The land on which the crops are planted and equipment also were lent by some Chicanos. The harvest is being divided among them and the volunteer workers, according to the needs of the family. Volunteers have come from all over the United States to help make this dream of working communally again and becoming self-sufficient real.

This is what we want: To run our own lives. To have the *sierra*, with its beautiful high green grass now going to waste, belong to the people again. To graze our animals like we used to, without any fences. To be able to go to the *sierra* freely to hunt deer or fish without anyone telling us what to do. To be able to go into the *sierra* and cut wood as needed.

We want good doctors and medical clinics that really want to cure people, not like the present doctors, who only care about money.

We are sick and tired of having someone tell us how many animals we can take into the mountains and when we can have meat to eat, while rich Texans throw meat away.

We are sick and tired of being considered "inferior" to the rich white race, and of white people telling us that our bronze race is ugly, ignorant, superstitious and lazy, and that our Indian ancestors were "savages."

We want to rule our own schools. We want to be taught in Spanish by good Chicano teachers who know as well as love and are proud of our Indian and Spanish heritage, culture and history.

Viva La Causa! Viva La Raza, our people!

Tierra o Muerte—the famous cry of the Zapatistas in the Mexican Revolution—Land or Death!

Hosea L. Williams, II

Fifteen-year-old Hosea Williams writes, "I have been actively involved in civil rights since I could walk and even before my parents took me and my sisters to meetings. I have been in all of the major marches including the famous Selma to Montgomery March of 1965 and the Meredith March. I spent the summer of 1968 in Resurrection City in Washington, D.C., and was jailed, along with the other poor people on the Mule Train, when it entered Georgia on the Southern Leg. I have been gassed in Mississippi, Savannah, Georgia, Birmingham, Alabama, and Washington, D.C., during peaceful demonstrations. I have no regrets, however. My entire life has been spent fighting with my father for black people's rights. I am anxiously awaiting the day when I can work full-time with my parents in this struggle for human dignity and equality for my people and all poor people. My greatest problem is not hating white people for the terrible beatings my father has received and for the long terms he has been forced to spend behind bars for asking for his God-given rights and the rights written in our Constitution. At times I am very bitter and my father has to caution me and my brothers and sisters not to judge others, lest we also be judged and found wanting. I am a product of the impatient generation and I don't intend to spend my life as a slave—I'd rather die fighting for my freedom."

✠✠✠✠✠✠✠✠✠✠✠✠✠✠✠✠✠✠✠✠✠✠✠✠✠✠✠✠✠✠✠✠

I feel that the main reason for riots during the summer is that living in those hot, dusty slum shacks a person must come outside in order to survive. And when people gather outside they start discussing their problems and whose fault it is that they live in such conditions. They may start talking about how hard they work and how little they get. Then they may think about how hard the black man has worked from the discovery of America up until today, a period of five centuries—too long for any race to have lived in an *earthly hell*. After they get talking about their troubles and listening to the problems of their ghetto neighbors, they may get the feeling that the only way to calm themselves is to take a drink. If that doesn't help much, they may take two or three more, and the result is often drunkenness. Then they think of violence as the only way to get back at the white segregationist who forces them to live and die in rat traps called "communities." Then the liquor store closes and they say they want another drink, and the only way to get it is to take it, so they break in. The police come along and the violence starts!

Another reason is that black men are turned into slum dwellers because of their inferior education. Because he lacks education, a black man cannot get a job, so he steals, kills and destroys private property in order to exist. I say *exist*, because even after he does these things, he is not actually *living*. When a man feels strongly that he wants a woman and she won't marry him, he may fall so low as to rape the woman he loves. When there is little money, a lot of men will drink before they eat. But there are some men who will look for jobs although they have only a third grade education. When they apply, a lot of times it turns out they don't have enough education to be even a garbage man or a manual street sweeper. And because of this, a man steals to keep his three-year-old son and his wife alive. When he is caught, the family fails. Many times a student's father can't get anything but a low-paying job so the high school student has to drop out of school and work so the family can survive.

We, the black youth of America, demand that after

every riot or disturbance of any kind a study committee should be set up: 75 percent of the committee
should be poor people from the community and 25
percent should be government officials. The reason for
having poor people comprise 75 percent of the committee is that they are best informed on the subject
of riots in their own community. And I think that if
the people of the community knew that the majority of
the committee were members of that community, they
would respect their decisions.

We, the black youth of America, demand that a
policeman should not be told to shoot a rioter on sight
during a riot. Why? Because anyone is liable to make
a mistake. When a policeman is told to shoot on sight,
he believes he has a license to shoot any one in the
area he thinks might be a rioter. If a human being is
killed by mistake, no one cares. The decision to shoot
is left entirely to a white, prejudiced, violent policeman, acting in the heat of confusing action.

We, the black youth of America, demand that heavy
artillery should not be used in our cities, unless the
government is expecting a black-against-white civil war.
Why? I believe something is wrong with a country
where a man with a coke bottle fights a man in a tank.
Today a governor has the authority to call in the National Guard with tanks, machine guns, etc. I do not
believe that one or two or even ten men have the right
to decide that one hundred or two hundred black men
should die.

We, the black youth of America, demand that tear
gas and mace not be used to dispurse a nonviolent
march. Some of the gasses used by the police have been
known to damage people's eyes, not temporarily, but
for their entire life. Many times gassing has forced
mothers to take their babies to the hospital. Also,
gasses are known to prove fatal to some small children.

Even during a riot the kind of gasses used should be thought about very carefully. Also the amount, because a lot of the gas used is blown by the wind and travels to harm innocent bystanders a block away.

We, the black youth of America, demand that only persons involved should be allowed to negotiate settlements after riots in the black community. By this I mean that only the people who know what it is all about can give the government a true picture of what is happening, what has happened and what is going to happen if the government doesn't do the right thing. In the past the government has decided whom they are going to negotiate with. Usually, they pick the Uncle Toms and Aunt Tomicenas. If the government continues to do this, it will never get a true picture or any right ideas on what to do. The people must elect whom they want to decide on what's to be done. The white man must realize this!

We, the black youth of America, demand that local leaders be allowed to assume more responsibility. After a riot, for instance, local leaders should be a part of the committee that decides how much money is to be spent in rebuilding the destroyed houses or private enterprises. They should also have a voice in deciding what needs to be done to prevent future riots. In the past the government has stopped the shooting and looting but never thought about how to stop the causes behind shooting and looting. I believe that I would riot less if my next door neighbor asked me to stop than if it were the mayor or anyone else having something to do with the government.

We, the black youth of America, demand that wild, killer dogs not be used in a riot. Weapons of the police department are supposed to be used to protect people, but the fact is dogs are used for killing or harming people. Police have been known to let their dogs (Ger-

man shepherds) loose in crowds of over two hundred
adults and very young children. I do not believe God
put dogs on this earth to be used to harm men.

We, the black youth of America, demand that after
white men's stores have been burned down, the government should provide enough money so some of the
black community can own the businesses from then on.
If a black man owns a store, he won't burn it down,
and his next door neighbor won't burn it down. And if
enough stores are owned by black men, there will be
fewer riots. We demand that the government provide
the money because it is the government's fault that we
have riots and it is their duty to prevent them.

We, the black youth of America, demand that a person should not be arrested and taken to jail just because
he or she is seen in the area of a riot. For instance,
when a person is three blocks away from a riot scene
and has long hair and a black leather jacket on with
maybe "Black Power" written on it, he should not be
identified or treated as a rioter. When a person is found
innocent of this or any other alleged crime, the government should be forced to call the victim's employer and
say that it was the government's fault that the employee missed those days from work, which in turn
forces the employer to pay the employee for missed
days. The government should then be forced to reimburse the employer for the money paid the employee.

I give you these demands in order to get across to
the American Establishment that the black youth of
America are tired of being forced to go some thousands
of miles overseas to fight useless battles that are killing
thousands of black men when there are much more
serious battles that must be fought and won right here
in America.

The battles that I am speaking of are those of poverty, ignorance, disease, education and unrest between

the blacks and whites of America. I don't believe riots will end until all of these and more battles have been fought and won here in this unjust country.

The war we should be fighting is here in America where the black man is still trying to free himself of the terrible murdering chains forced upon him by the white man. The reason the white man keeps the black man in slavery is because he is afraid. He is afraid to free the man he has kept down for so long. He is afraid this man will seek revenge. He is afraid that the black man will treat the white man as the white man has treated him. But now we, the black youth of America, say to you that we shall not stand for the injustices that our forefathers put up with and we demand that that you truly free us all at last.

Raphael Zahler

A twenty-five-year-old native of New York, Raphael
Zahler graduated Phi Beta Kappa from Harvard and is
now working for his doctorate at the University of
Chicago. He has worked in Mississippi, Alabama and
Georgia for the Southern Christian Leadership Conference and the Scope Project, from the earliest sit-ins
through voter registration campaigns. Active in the
U. of C. Hillel foundation, he has conducted services
there and at his home synagogue.

✠✠✠✠✠✠✠✠✠✠✠✠✠✠✠✠✠✠✠✠✠✠✠✠✠✠

We are committed, concerned Jewish youth. We
have studied both the Talmud and Franz Rosenzweig;
we read *Commentary* as well as *The Village Voice*. We
are religiously observant, Hillel activists, Zionist youth
leaders. We love our religion and our people.

And we are sickened by the spiritual poverty of the
American Jewish organizations. We are amazed at the
social unconcern of large segments of our community;
we are shocked by those who take a narrow view of
"what is good for the Jews" and thereby slip into white
blacklash and worse. We have long since grown tired
of the sterility of our home congregations, and we are
ashamed of the intellectual vapidity that made *Portnoy's Complaint* a best seller but Martin Buber a largely
forgotten man. We read in the papers of endless fund-
raising dinners, yet when we complain that the Jewish
organizations are unresponsive to youth, we are called
lost, infantile or even anti-Semitic—our reward for trying to dedicate ourselves to our Jewish heritage in the
midst of the modern world.

These are the feelings of a large and growing group of Jewish youth, people who have tried to remain sensitive to currents of ideas in both the secular and the Jewish world. These feelings are not caused by a sense of complete alienation from Judaism or from society at large. They simply express the bitter disappointment of dedicated young Jews at the discrepancies between practice and preachment: in a word, hypocrisy. Of course, many Jewish agencies do live up to the highest prophetic traditions, like the Jewish Peace Fellowship or the National Jewish Organizing Project. We admire the work of the Hillel foundations and the many Jewish charities and civil liberties groups. But, by and large, the colossus that is sometimes called the "Jewish Establishment" continues to drive more and more youth away from Judaism.

Consider first of all the political posture of the Jewish Establishment. Unlike most of today's youth, most Jewish groups are concerned above all not with poverty or war or exploitation, but with anti-Semitism. Visions of anti-Semites hiding behind every tree distract their attention from other things. Why is it, for example, that the organizations that have struggled so energetically for oppressed Soviet Jewry never mention the Jews of neo-Nazi South Africa? Many American Jews are proud that Mrs. Helen Suzman, heroine of the antiapartheid forces, happens to be of Jewish stock; few are aware that the ruling bodies of South African Jewry have repeatedly endorsed their government's genocidal policies. One Jewish layman, concerned about organized Judaism's nearly total silence on apartheid compared to the protests of some Christian counterparts both within South Africa and outside, wrote to a wide spectrum of American Jewish leaders about it. The most polite told him that it was dangerous to risk getting the South African government angry at its

Jewish citizens; the others told him to mind his own business.

Moral issues aside, would the same "don't rock the boat" attitude have saved Germany's Jews in 1938? The urge to make the world safe for Judaism, regardless of the moral consequences, probably led to the resolution of organized Orthodox Jewry in support of the war in Vietnam a few years ago, or more recently, to the helmeted commandos of the Jewish Defense League. The latter group combines reactionary political views with paramilitary tactics. But nearly all the Jewish leaders who are so quick to condemn extremism on the left have carefully avoided mentioning these right-wing zealots.

These extreme attitudes reflect a hypersensitivity to purported anti-Semitism and a misguided approach for resisting it that deeply disturb Jewish youth. Most of our personal experiences bear out the conclusions of the National Jewish Community Relations Advisory Council: "Overt anti-Semitism continues at a low ebb." More important, our response to the anti-Semitism that does exist should be based not on narrow grounds of self-interest, but rather on a desire to eliminate all persecution. As Emil Fackenheim has expressed it, when our memories of the European holocaust cause us to cringe from today's tyrants, we give Hitler a posthumous victory. On the contrary, we are commanded, both by the blood of the six million and by the unchanging voice of our God, to fight all oppression, to rebuke even our brothers when they do wrong.

Even the most self-interested Jew, before he rushes to his mimeograph machine to denounce the latest black militant, should consider in "practical" terms the failure of the Jewish defense agencies in pre-Hitler Germany. Dr. Trude Weis-Rosmarin, in an article called "How NOT to Fight Antisemitism," points out that anti-Semitism is an irrational force; it will not go away if the Jews try to "behave themselves" as in South Africa. The Jew who cooperates with the executioner will find his head on the chopping block next; Jews will be safe only when all minorities are. Denouncing anti-Semites and suppressing their propaganda is even more unwise: "The experience of the German Jews documents that these are Pyrrhic victories," comments Dr. Weis-Rosmarin.

Unfortunately, in the New York school crisis Jewish leaders followed the fears of those whom they were supposed to be leading. Sociologist Herbert Gans has warned, "There is a danger that Jews will develop the same over-reaction to the black rhetoric and the black demand for equal rights that has emerged among poor and sub-affluent whites in recent years." Indeed, the teachers' union reprinted thousands of copies of a few sheets of anti-Semitic propaganda, the shock wave spread, the Jewish organizations fell in line and the panic was on. Ardent civil libertarians now tried to censor radio station WBAI; dispassionate observations by the Jewish sociologist Nathan Glazer, in the mouth of a black schoolgirl, became hard-core anti-Semitism, and the New York Board of Rabbis tried to oust the city's first effective human rights commissioner for being soft on anti-Semitism. The low point, it seems to me, was reached in the shameful *Commentary* article by Milton Himmelfarb, which solemnly proclaimed the rise of a secret WASP–Negro conspiracy to get the Jews, who would be well-advised to fight for their lives. If contemporary Jewry is best represented by this kind of snivelling moral bankruptcy, blind to the sufferings of others, it deserves to be superseded by a generation more aware of the prophetic commands "to loose the fetters of wickedness, to undo the bands of the yoke, and to let the oppressed go free, and that ye break every yoke."

Amos cried, " 'Are you not as the children of the Ethiopians unto me, O children of Israel?' saith the Lord." But the Anti-Defamation League readies its big guns against discriminatory private clubs while Jewish slumlords defame their people by letting their tenants' children die of lead poisoning. Philanthropists congratulate themselves on donations to hospitals, while police continue to gun down ghetto youths with impunity—youths who are dead on arrival at the shiny new emergency room. Jews are proud of their liberal voting record, but white Jewish ward committeemen still control all-black Chicago neighborhoods. Meanwhile, Jewish citizens, proud of their yearly ten-dollar contribution to the NAACP, feel entitled to write letters beginning, "I've always stood for civil rights, but . . . " Indeed, Jewish organizations have been free recently with statements harshly criticizing black leaders, but as Roy Innis complains, "let a black leader criticize Israel or a Jewish group, and he automatically becomes anti-Semitic."

I will be accused, I suppose, of demanding that Jews be better than everyone else. And, in fact, I do think it is obscene that a people which has suffered so unspeakably from race hatred should make peace with, let alone profit from, the oppression of any other race.

The fact is that Jewish individuals are still in the forefront of the fight for racial justice, but the Jewish organizations have slipped into a torpid gradualism, or no movement at all. In Boston not long ago a notorious Jewish slumlord was brought before a Beth Din, a Jewish religious court, and told that his exploitation of the poor was forbidden by classical Jewish law. How many other Jewish organizations have acted to fight the Jewish-owned grocery chain that sells rotten meat in the ghetto, or even to help the desperate Jewish merchant move to a more hospitable area? Which Jewish leaders challenged Mayor Loeb of Memphis in the days before Martin Luther King was murdered, and which groups have supported rent strikes, boycotts or other action projects? How many rabbis—and how many laymen— have rebuked their bigoted friends who mutter about the *schwartze* after they listen to the annual brother-hood-week sermon? We must strive to make prejudice as un-Jewish a quality as drunkenness traditionally was. Jewish groups must take the lead in new educational projects to end bigotry in the white community, to halt "blockbusting" and create stable intergrated areas, and to put money and talent into action to rebuild and reinvigorate the ghettos, following the lead of Chicago's Jewish Council on Urban Affairs. This is doing "what's good for the Jews" in the broad sense: establishing a society where no group is mistreated.

The organized Jewish community has not lived up to its social responsibilities in the eyes of many committed Jewish young people, so it is not surprising that its official relations with youth are frustrating to all concerned. Those who suggest putting more honest facts into the pablum that is contemporary Jewish education, for example, are not heard. Many of my friends talk casually about how they outgrew their Hebrew school years. Perhaps the reason is that Jewish after-school programs face the impossible job of teaching Jewish-ness to grade school youngsters whose homes are empty of Jewishness. Without a meaningful Jewish atmos-phere provided by parents, a part-time teacher of younger children can be little more than a baby-sit-ter. Worse, when Jewish youths approach Bar Mitzvah age and become ready to understand deeper ideas, they lose interest in the shallow approach of Hebrew school and wind up thinking of the Jewish tradition as a bunch of odd rituals and Bible stories.

Let the caterers worry about training Bar Mitzvah boys. We spend time and money to develop programs that reach older, more mature young people: uncompromising study of the difficult ethical problems in the Bible, significant modern Jewish philosophers like Buber and Rosenzweig, the dynamics of the classical texts and the liturgy, and the possibility of Jewish participation in the social revolution of our time. Otherwise Jewish youth will continue to regard Judaism as something to be outgrown.

The failure to deal with the urgent needs of youth reaches into other areas. Those who ask the organizations of American Jewry for help with draft counseling or a Jewish theological basis for conscientious objection are frequently turned away; those who organize against oppression, like the Jews for Urban Justice, are mocked by the Jewish press. *Response*, a magazine published by Jewish college students, discusses the Jewish power structure in tones ranging from harsh: "The establishment is undemocratic, unrepresentative, irrelevant, and a real danger to the welfare of American Jews," to mild: "The religious community will have to be more vigorous in its articulation and its actualization of moral imperatives." The basic dissatisfaction is the same.

But these statements and others like them remain largely unheard. Jewish student leaders repeated them again and again at a recent national conference on Jewish college youth, and for every community representative who sympathized, there were several who closed their shells. A noted rabbi, writing in the *Chicago Jewish Sentinal*, decided that the students must have been "off on trips of their own, God-knows-where," "too preoccupied with the pangs of toilet training or adolescence," or "too busy reading *Superman* or *Mad* "to be aware of the great achievements of the American Jewish community. This kind of friendly mudslinging is common wherever dedicated, Jewishly educated youths have the nerve to suggest that some Jewish groups have sold out on their liberal commitments.

Those few Jewish community leaders who are sensitive to youth—and their names are bywords among young Jewish artivists—can bear witness to the exciting emergence of large numbers of committed, informed, socially activist Jewish youths, rooted in their Jewishness and aware of its many meanings, yet sharing in the agonies of secular America. They are torn in this two-way stretch between the universal and the particular commitment in their friendships, in their politics, in their values and in their deepest emotions. This tension can be cruelly painful, but it can also be dynamic and creative, blending the best of both outlooks with exciting results. We need more people who can take their stand as Jews confidently, in the middle of the conflicts of society, and relate to the Jewish world with a deep understanding of the non-Jewish community.

Resolving the tension of this two-way stretch by cutting one's ties to the outside world often leads to a frantic and self-destructive retreat inward. The other extreme is a complete rejection of everything Jewish. Either cop-out is disastrous for the community; yet those in power who inadvertently force us to choose between these two extremes make the dilemma worse. There should be no conflict of loyalties between Judaism and secular involvement: a student activist is not someone lost to Judaism, neither is a person who questions religious values in the course of his searching. Jews need not keep American society at arms' length to remain

Jews, if they are secure in their own identity. If we have the strength to continue grappling with this creative tension, we will produce a new generation of Jews that all men will be proud of. And it is in the interest of all Jews that we do precisely that.

The Unanimous Declaration of Interdependence

When, in the course of evolution, it becomes necessary for one species to denounce the notion of independence from all the rest and to assume among the powers of the earth, the interdependent station to which the natural laws of the cosmos have placed them, a decent respect for the opinions of all mankind requires that they should declare the conditions which impel them to assert their interdependence.

We hold these truths to be self-evident—that all species have evolved with equal and unalienable rights; that among these are Life, Liberty and the pursuit of Happiness. That to insure these rights, nature has instituted certain principles for the sustenance of all species, deriving these principles from the capabilities of the planet's life-support system. That whenever any behavior by members of one species becomes destructive of these principles, it is the function of other members of that species to alter or abolish such behavior and to reestablish the theme of interdependence with all life, in such a form and in accordance with those natural principles, that will effect their safety and happiness. Prudence, indeed, will dictate that cultural values long established should not be altered for light and transient causes, that mankind is more disposed to suffer from asserting a vain notion of independence than to right themselves by abolishing that culture to which they are now accustomed. But when a long train of abuses and usurpations of these principles of interdependence, evinces a subtle design to reduce them, through absolute despoliation of the planet's fertility, to a state of ill will, bad health, and great anxiety, it is their right, it is their duty, to throw off such notions of independence from other species and from the life support system, and to provide new guards for the reestablishment of the security and maintenance of these principles. Such has been the outlet and patient suffrage of all species, and such is now the necessity which constrains the species Homo sapiens to reassert the principles of interdependence. The history of the present notion of independence is a history of repeated injuries and usurpations, all having in direct effect the establishment of an absolute tyranny over Life. To prove this, let facts be submitted to a candid world.

1. People have refused to recognize the roles of other species and the importance of natural principles for growth of the food they require.

2. People have refused to recognize that they are interacting with other species in an evolutionary process.

3. People have failed the waters that all life partakes of.

4. People have transformed the face of the earth to enhance their notion of independence from it, and in so doing have interrupted many natural processes that they are dependent upon.

5. People have contaminated the common household with substances that are foreign to the life processes which are causing many organisms great difficulties.

6. People have massacred and extincted fellow species for their feathers and furs, for their skins and tusks.

7. People have persecuted most persistantly those known as coyote, lion, wolf and fox because of their dramatic role in the expression of interdependence.

8. People are proliferating in such an irresponsible manner as to threaten the survival of all species.

9. People have warred upon one another, which has brought great sorrow to themselves and vast destruction to the homes and the food supplies of many living things.

People have denied others the right to live to completion their interdependencies to the full extent of their capabilities.

We, therefore, among the mortal representatives of the eternal process of life and evolutionary principles, in mutual humbleness, explicitly stated, appealing to the ecological consciousness of the world for the rectitude of our intentions, do solemnly publish and declare that all species are interdependent; that they are all free to realize these relationships to the full extent of their capabilities; that each species is subservient to the requirements of the natural processes that sustain all life. And for the support of this declaration, with a firm reliance on all other members of our species who understand their consciousness as a capability, we mutually pledge to assist all of us and our brothers to interact in order to realize a life process that manifests its maximum potential of diversity, vitality and planetary fertility to ensure the continuing of life on earth.